WEAPON

THE GATLING GUN

PETER SMITHURST

Series Editor Martin Pegler

First published in Great Britain in 2015 by Osprey Publishing,
PO Box 883, Oxford, OX1 9PL, UK
PO Box 3985, New York, NY 10185-3985, USA
E-mail: info@ospreypublishing.com

Osprey Publishing is part of the Osprey Group

A CIP catalogue record for this book is available from the British
Library

Print ISBN: 978 1 4728 0597 3
PDF ebook ISBN: 978 1 4728 0598 0
ePub ebook ISBN: 978 1 4728 0599 7

Index by Mark Swift
Typeset in Sabon and Univers
Battlescenes by Johnny Shumate
Originated by PDQ Media, Bungay, UK
Printed in China through Worldprint Ltd

15 16 17 18 19   10 9 8 7 6 5 4 3 2 1

Osprey Publishing is supporting the Woodland Trust, the UK's
leading woodland conservation charity, by funding the dedication
of trees.

www.ospreypublishing.com

The NRA Museums
Since 1935, the NRA Museum collection has become one of the
world's finest museum collections dedicated to firearms. Now
housed in three locations, the NRA Museums offer a glimpse into
the firearms that built our nation, helped forge our freedom, and
captured our imagination. The **National Firearms Museum**,
located at the NRA Headquarters in Fairfax, Virginia, details and
examines the nearly 700-year history of firearms with a special
emphasis on firearms, freedom, and the American experience.
The **National Sporting Arms Museum**, at the Bass Pro Shops in
Springfield, Missouri, explores and exhibits the historical
development of hunting arms in America from the earliest
explorers to modern day, with a focus on hunting, conservation,
and freedom. The **Frank Brownell Museum of the Southwest**, at
the NRA Whittington Center in Raton, NM, is a jewel box
museum with 200 guns that tells the history of the region from
the earliest Native American inhabitants through early Spanish
exploration, the Civil War, and the Old West. For more
information on the NRA Museums and hours, visit www.
NRAmuseums.com.

Dedicated to the memory of H.J. (Herb) Woodend, custodian of
the MOD Pattern Room until it closed. His untimely death
deprived many firearms historians of a great friend and a wealth
of knowledge and wisdom.

Acknowledgements
Very few factual books, especially those touching upon historical
subjects, can be written without the help of others, past and
present. The bibliography indicates the heavy reliance placed
upon both earlier and more recent writers and commentators.
However, to leave it at that would not do justice to those of the
present day who have given invaluable help and support in
various ways and for which they have my special thanks and
gratitude: trustees and colleagues of Royal Armouries, notably
Chris Streek, Stuart Ivinson and James Avison in the library,
Alison Watson, Curatorial Manager, and Lisa Traynor, Assistant
Curator, Firearms; Alex MacKenzie, Curator, and Richard
Colton, Historian, Springfield Armory National Historic Site,
Springfield, Massachusetts; Edward Hull; Joe Moran and Evan
Sikes, Cowan's Auctions, Inc., Cincinnati, Ohio; J. Wesley Dillon
of James D. Julia, Inc. (Auctions), Fairfield, Maine; Janice
Murray, Director, and Shane Bartley, Commercial Manager,
National Army Museum, London for taking time to supply
images in the midst of reorganization; Joss Grandeau, Twin Falls,
Idaho; David Alderson; Rob Brassington for supplying images
from his excellent series of animated gun mechanisms; Tony
Watts; and Steve Fjestad, Blue Book Publications, Inc.,
Minneapolis, Minnesota. Finally, any errors are my responsibility.
As Thomas Jefferson said, 'He who knows nothing is closer to the
truth than he whose mind is filled with falsehoods and errors.'

Editor's note
In this book linear, weight, and volume measurements are given
in imperial units of measurement (yards, feet, inches, pounds,
ounces, grains). The exception is weapons calibre, where metric is
used in some cases, depending on the context. Where imperial
units of measurement differ from US customary, the former are
used in the text. The following data will help when converting
between imperial and metric measurements:

1yd = 91.44cm	1oz = 28.35g
1ft = 30.48cm	1 grain = 0.002oz
1in = 2.54cm	1 grain = 0.065g
1lb = 453.59kg	

Front cover, above: The Model 1883 Gatling, unlike earlier
models which relied on gravity ammunition-feed systems, was
fitted with Accles' Positive Feed. This allowed extremes of
elevation and depression to be handled easily using the simple
'pointer bar' and enabled rates of fire from 800 to 1,500 rounds
per minute depending on whether the crank handle operated
through gears as when fitted to the side, or fitted directly to the
mainshaft at the rear. Such rates of fire required the gun's
mechanism to be substantially strengthened.
(NRA Museums, NRAmuseums.com)
Front cover, below: A Naval Brigade Gatling in action in the
streets of Alexandria. Only 'warning shots' over the heads of the
rioters were fired to prevent a massacre, which showed great
restraint on the part of the sailors. *Illustrated London News*,
29 July 1882, p. 101. (Private collection)
Title page: Prussian soldiers examine a captured Gatling gun.
Every Saturday, 22 October 1870, p. 673. (Private collection)

CONTENTS

INTRODUCTION

Since the first firearms appeared there have been continuous attempts to improve their 'effectiveness'. Effectiveness can mean many things. The gradual transition from the crude hand cannon in which the propellant was ignited by a piece of smouldering match cord held in the hand, through the matchlock where the human hand was replaced by a mechanical 'hand' activated by a trigger; then the technological quantum leap forward to the wheel-lock, in which sparks were generated mechanically at the instant of firing. Then came the much simpler flintlock, where the sparks were created by flint striking steel. Finally, came the allying of another chemical process to the burning of gunpowder – the ability of some sensitive chemicals to detonate when struck and provide the flame to ignite the charge. These are all impressive developments in the effectiveness of firearms. Then we have the simple transition from a smoothbore barrel firing a plain spherical ball to the rifled barrel where a series of spiral grooves in its bore make a pointed, elongated bullet spin in flight – its shape, giving it less air resistance, its tight fit in the bore to make full use of the force of the explosion and the fact that it has gyroscopic stability from its rapid spinning combine to give it far greater range and accuracy over the old round ball. These also are impressive additions to 'effectiveness'. But we should not deceive ourselves by hiding behind terminology. The bottom line of effectiveness in a military firearm is to kill or wound as many of the enemy on the battlefield as quickly as possible.

By the middle years of the 19th century, firearms were on the threshold of perhaps their biggest evolutionary step of all – the development of breechloading and the self-contained cartridge which together provide the foundations of all modern firearms. By that time also, the limited mechanization of a variety of previously manual manufacturing processes – especially in the textile, and iron and steel, manufacturing industries – was an established fact. But in the United States, where manufacturing had been stifled under colonial rule and labour was thin on the ground and expensive, after Independence 'Yankee ingenuity' was applied to taking mechanizing to new levels on the farm, in the home and in the factory. Once established, Eli Whitney's cotton gin became indispensable to the processing of raw cotton. At the Crystal Palace Exhibition in 1851, Cyrus McCormick unveiled his reaper for harvesting wheat. It would not be long before the sewing machine began to appear in the home. By this time also the application of machinery to all the operations in manufacturing firearms had been brought to perfection. It should not be surprising to find that this same 'Yankee ingenuity' turned towards mechanizing the process of loading and firing guns also.

The arrival of a reliable self-contained cartridge allowed the development of a variety of repeating firearms in which cartridges were fed into the breech by a lever-operated mechanism which opened the breech, extracted an empty cartridge case, fed in a replacement, closed the breech and at the same time cocked the gun ready for firing when the trigger was pulled. Early examples of this type of system are the Henry and Spencer rifles of the 1860s. What if the separate actions of loading and firing could be combined so that in a single operation, the gun could be loaded, cocked and fired in a repetitive cycle *and* could have an unlimited supply of ammunition? Such a mechanized gun would deliver awesome firepower.

The first step along this pathway was a weapon that came to be known as the 'Union Repeating Gun' or the Ager 'Coffee Mill' gun on account of its ammunition feed hopper. It was tested by the US Ordnance Department in 1861 and a limited number were actually purchased, but it was not a great success. The weapon fired standard .58in-calibre paper cartridges

Ager 'Coffee Mill' gun, .58in calibre, serial no. 2, manufactured by Woodward & Cox, New York; the hopper is marked 'E. NUGENT N.Y.'. This weapon is named after Wilson Ager, but there is some uncertainty as to when the Ager gun was invented and, indeed, whether he was actually the inventor. This doubt may also have sprung from the fact that UK patent no. 24 (1862) is in the name of E. Nugent, the same that appears on the hopper of the example shown here. However, the same weapon appears under Ager's name in UK patent no. 152 (1866), which does nothing to clarify the situation. (Courtesy US National Park Service, Springfield Armory National Historic Site; photograph James Langone, Springfield. SPAR 5612)

Originally in .50-70 Government calibre, but later converted to .45-70 Government calibre, this Gatling gun is mounted on the later 1877-style carriage. The rectangular brass maker's plate reads 'Gatling Battery Gun #22 Patented May 3, 1865. Colt's Patent Firearms Manufacturing Co. Hartford, Conn, U.S.A.'. Only two others of this model are thought to exist. This gun was purchased by the US Navy in 1866 and installed on USS *Yorktown* (Gun Boat No. 1), remaining on board until she was decommissioned in 1919. Seeing extensive service in foreign waters 'showing the flag', *Yorktown* had numerous engagements in the China Sea during the 1890s and patrolled South American and Mexican waters prior to World War I and then US coastal waters towards the end of the war. The gun was then donated to the Houston Museum, Texas. In 1967 the museum sold the gun at public auction to a Houston collector; the collector restored and cared for the gun until 1991 (Cowan's Auctions 2007: 82–83). However, it shows various anomalies, most notably the vertical magazine, which may be the result of conversion to the .45-70 cartridge, and what appears to be a lock-removal plug, which did not appear until the 1869 (UK) or 1871 (US) patents. That may also be a result of later improvement but would have entailed changing the drive mechanism from bevel wheels to worm-and-pinion, otherwise there would not have been clearance for the bolt to be withdrawn if the patent drawings are any guide. (Photograph courtesy of Cowan's Auctions, Cincinnati, Ohio)

which were placed inside steel cartridge casings closed at one end and fitted with a percussion nipple. Like all such guns which used pre-loaded chambers with an external percussion cap, at the instant of firing the chamber had to be pressed very tightly against the breech face of the barrel to avoid gas leakage, then released so it could fall away and be replaced by the next one. Gradually, wear and tear would take their toll and obturation, the seal between breech and barrel, was compromised with the increased risk of flame from the explosion escaping and igniting the charges in the cartridges waiting in the hopper. Another important consideration was that it only had one barrel and while it functioned beautifully using empty chambers, as Major G.V. Fosbery VC – himself a firearms innovator – pointed out in 1869 when the gun was tested in Britain:

> the only thing forgotten seemed to be that when using loaded chambers, and firing at the rate of 100 discharges per minute, the flame of 7,500 grains of powder, and nearly 7lbs of lead would pass through this single barrel in that time. The effect on trial proved to be that the barrel grew first red and then nearly white hot, large drops of fused metal poured from the muzzle, and the firing had to be discontinued for fear of worse consequences. (Fosbery 1869: 543)

But a train of thinking had been set in motion and was not lost on Richard Jordan Gatling. He created what became probably the most easily recognized generic series of guns which even today, long after other manual rapid-fire guns were made obsolete by Hiram Maxim's invention of the fully automatic machine gun in 1883, find a place in modern military armament.

DEVELOPMENT
A new species of weapon is born

ORIGINS

Although not an engineer or gunmaker, Richard Jordan Gatling, like many of his fellow Americans, was 'an interested amateur'. He embodied much of what Alexander Hamilton, first Secretary of the Treasury in the newly independent United States of America and 'Father of American Manufacturing', commented upon: 'If there be anything in a remark often to be met with, namely, that there is, in the genius of the people of this country, a peculiar aptitude for mechanic improvements ...' (Hamilton 1827: 22). It is worth remembering that at that time there was no such thing as an 'engineer' and most of the world's technological advances – the industrial revolution in all its varied forms – had been accomplished by amateur 'dabblers' and 'tinkerers' fired by unbridled imagination and a belief that things could be done in different and better ways.

Gatling was born in 1818 on a remote farm at Maney's Neck near Murfreesboro in North Carolina. His attendance at school was probably restricted to the winter months, when he and his fellow pupils were not needed to help on the farms, and confined to the essentials so that by the time his schooling was finished at 16 years of age he was literate and numerate. But he received informal and equally valuable education on the farm. He was part of a family of 'dabblers and tinkerers'. His father, Jordan Gatling, was a self-taught blacksmith and carpenter, essential skills to keep a remote farm and household operational, and which had led him to obtain two patents in 1835 for a cotton thinner and cotton seed planter. Much later, in 1873, his brother James Henry constructed a flying machine which travelled 100ft before crashing into a tree.

7

Richard Jordan Gatling (1818–1903) is depicted in this photograph by celebrated photographer Mathew B. Brady (1822–96). What led Gatling to develop his gun? He was neither an engineer nor a gunmaker. According to a letter written to a friend in 1877 while residing in Indianapolis, his invention had been inspired by humanitarian needs: 'In 1861, during the opening events of the war I witnessed almost daily the departure of troops to the front and the return of the wounded, sick and dead. The most of the latter lost their lives, not in battle, but by sickness and exposure incident to the service. It occurred to me if I could invent a machine – a gun – which could by its rapidity of fire, enable one man to do as much battle duty as a hundred, that it would, to a great extent, supersede the necessity of large armies, and consequently, exposure to battle and disease be greatly diminished' (quoted in Keller 2008: 27). One can possibly discern here the beginnings of a concept that was to dominate the world a century later – a deterrent, not just superseding the necessity for large armies but of giving warfare itself unthinkable consequences. (Library of Congress)

By degrees the young Gatling added his father's practical skills to his own accomplishments. So much so, that when he was 18 years old he had responded to a plea from the US Government to find a better way of propelling ships than paddle wheels and oars and took his model of a screw propeller to the Patent Office in Washington, DC. There he was told he was just too late, a patent having been granted to John Ericsson a few weeks previously. Had he not delayed, waiting for winter to give way to better weather in the spring, it would be his name we associate with the invention. Richard Jordan Gatling's dabbling and tinkering was to bring him over 50 patents, his first in 1844 for a wheat-seed sower and his last in 1902 for a steam plough.

THE MODELS OF 1862

There seems to be a degree of confusion in the designation of various guns depending upon the changes that were made in their construction and functional characteristics. How far these were based on changes in the gun's basic mechanism and mechanical components or on the ammunition

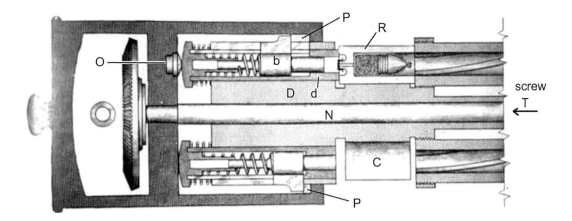

feed systems used is equally uncertain in some cases. The invention that put Gatling on the path to worldwide fame was US patent no. 36,836 of 4 November 1862, simply titled 'Machine Gun'. In creating his gun, Gatling incorporated a pre-loaded iron or steel 'cartridge', a cylinder closed at one end and fitted with a nipple for a percussion cap, which had been used in the Ager. Such a device was not new to Ager and had been used before; it was the simplest way of achieving what was required. But far from copying the Ager, Gatling introduced several important features which were to remain through the whole series of weapons and characterize these guns. Top of the list was the fact that it was multibarrelled. It was therefore less likely to suffer the overheating problem recounted in regard to the Ager. Allied to this was the fact that each barrel had its own individual firing mechanism, so even if one became faulty, the gun could still keep firing, albeit, in motor-car parlance, not on all cylinders.

All of the functional elements were carried on a central shaft set in a metal framework. First there was the cluster of barrels, usually six or ten; behind the barrels was a cartridge carrier; behind the cartridge carrier was the lock housing, which carried a number of locks or bolts corresponding with the number of barrels; and lastly there was a gear wheel which engaged with a gear on the crank handle on the side of the frame. All these elements were securely fixed to the shaft in such a way that they could not rotate independently, but equally importantly, to ensure that the lock housing and cartridge carrier were in correct alignment with the bore of the barrels.

After producing a prototype, in 1862 Gatling moved to Cincinnati, Ohio, where he placed an order with Miles H. Greenwood to have six guns manufactured. Unfortunately, before they could be delivered, the guns, drawings and patterns were destroyed in a fire at the factory. He then had another 12 guns manufactured by another Cincinnati company: McWhinney, Rindge, & Co. Throughout this period, Gatling continued to demonstrate his first gun, made while he was in Indianapolis, to

Detail of the lock mechanism showing a pre-loaded chamber (R) in position in the cartridge carrier (C) and about to be fired. As the barrel/lock assembly rotated, the head of the lock (d) was brought into contact with a raised 'button' (O) on the diaphragm which forced the lock forward slightly, pressing the cartridge chamber (R) tightly up against the mouth of the barrel. During this rotation, a projection on the hammer, or striker (b), rode against the inclined surface of a ring (P) encircling the lock carrier (D) and which acted as a cam. The inclined rear face of this ring caused the hammer (b) to be forced back against a spring and when the cartridge was in place and pressed against the mouth of the barrel, the projection on the hammer came to a step in the inclined plane, allowing the spring to drive it forward and strike the cap on the cartridge and thus firing it. Gatling noted in his patent 'an adjusting screw, T, is placed opposite the forward end of the shaft, N, for regulating the pressure on the cartridge chambers, K'. Note the use of bevel gears – a crown wheel and pinion – for the drive mechanism. Adapted from Chinn 1951: 49. (Private collection)

many army officers of rank and distinction, all of whom were highly pleased at the result of its performance. The American press of 1862

Model 1862 Gatling Gun Type II, adapted to fire the .58in rimfire metallic cartridge. Manufactured by McWhinney, Rindge, & Co., Cincinnati, Ohio, in 1863. This is probably identical to the one demonstrated in the Washington Navy Yard in 1863. (Courtesy US National Park Service, Springfield Armory National Historic Site; photograph James Langone, Springfield. SPAR 5613)

and 1863 teemed with accounts of these trials, and during all this period, no notice of a similar weapon, or at least none equalling or approaching the 'Gatling Battery' in the rapidity of its firing, appeared in any of the papers published in America or Europe. (Gatling 1870: 506)

As already noted, these first guns had ammunition consisting of pre-loaded steel chambers fitted with a percussion cap. However, the period of Gatling's innovation was also a time of innovation in ammunition and saw the development and increasing adoption of the self-contained metallic cartridge in America and, later, in other countries too. Without having to substantially alter his original design, Gatling adapted his pre-loaded steel chambers by simply boring them all the way through so that they could accept a metallic cartridge. It might be noted that on these guns the front sight was mounted on a bridge over the barrel cluster, allowing the gun to fire on 'top dead centre'.

During 1862 and 1863, the gun underwent various demonstrations and in March 1863, Major General Horatio G. Wright, in command of the Department of the Ohio, wrote to Brigadier General J.W. Ripley, Chief of Ordnance, suggesting that 'As a device for obtaining a heavy fire of small arms with very few men, it seems to me admirably adapted to transport steamers plying upon the Western rivers, where infantry squads are needed for security, against guerrilla and other predatory bands' (quoted in Gatling 1870: 508) and that Mr Rindge, agent for the

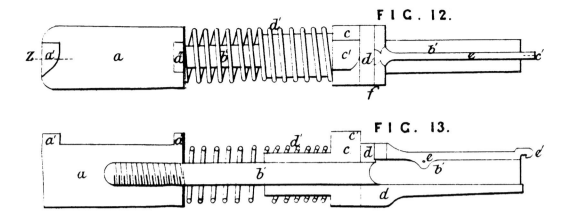

FIG. 12.

FIG. 13.

gun, be given the opportunity to demonstrate it. This is not only a commentary of the virtues of the gun, it is also a telling testimony to the perils faced by western settlements when civil war was added to frontier lawlessness.

After tests at the Navy Yard in Washington, DC, it was reported to Rear Admiral J.A.B. Dahlgren, head of US Navy Ordnance, in May 1863 that 'The gun or battery has stood the limited test given it admirably; has proved itself to be a very efficient arm at short range; is well constructed and calculated to stand the usage to which it would necessarily be subjected. It is suggested that an improvement in the manner of rifling the barrels would be advantageous' (Gatling 1870: 508). Gatling followed this advice by having a new set of barrels with altered rifling made and fitted and in June of that year a further series of tests was conducted at the Washington Navy Yard. Dahlgren was so impressed with their performance that he gave permission to commanders of fleets and squadrons to order guns for their commands, but few were actually supplied on account of Gatling's inability to have them manufactured speedily and in quantity.

THE MODEL OF 1865

Gatling realized that the use of bored-through chambers to enable the gun to use metallic cartridges was acceptable as a temporary measure, but to ensure the gun's future success a complete redesign of its fundamental mechanism was required to allow the gun to handle metallic cartridges directly without the need for an intermediary chamber. A consideration of what was required will illustrate that this was not a simple matter. With the early guns, the chambers, whether the percussion-cap variety or those made to accept metallic cartridges, simply dropped into the gun from a magazine at the top; the bolts were pushed forward slightly to force the chamber against the mouth of the barrel to achieve a degree of gas-seal, and the striker was pulled backwards and released to fire them. After firing, the now empty chambers simply dropped out of the gun at the bottom.

Details from the patent drawing showing the construction of the new bolt, or 'lock', assembly. UK patent no. 790 of 1865; US patent no. 47,631 of 1865. After a cartridge was fed into the cartridge carrier, the lock was driven forward by the lug (a^1) on the bolt 'head' or 'butt piece' (a) riding in an inclined elliptical cam groove on the inside of the lock casing. This caused the cartridge to be fed into the chamber of the barrel. When the cartridge was fully inserted, another cam, the 'cocking ring', in the forward part of the lock casing engaged with the lug (c^1) on the 'hammer' (c), pulling it backwards against the spring (d^1) and then releasing it, allowing the hammer to fly forwards and fire the cartridge. As the assembly continued to rotate, the lug (a^1) now encountered the elliptical cam groove as it changed direction towards the rear of the casing, causing the lock to move backwards, at the same time pulling the spent cartridge case out of the chamber by means of the extractor hooked over the rim of the case. And thus the process was repeated for each barrel in a continuous cycle. (Private collection)

11

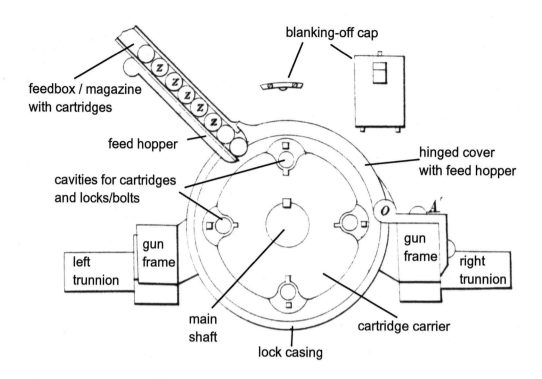

- blanking-off cap
- feedbox / magazine with cartridges
- feed hopper
- cavities for cartridges and locks/bolts
- hinged cover with feed hopper
- left trunnion
- gun frame
- gun frame
- right trunnion
- main shaft
- cartridge carrier
- lock casing

What was needed now was a sequence of much more complex events. The chambers to hold the cartridge now became part of the barrel, so cartridges had to be pushed forward a distance corresponding to their length so that they entered the chamber in the barrel; after firing, the empty cartridge cases then had to be withdrawn from the chamber. Thus there was a significant increase in the distance the bolt had to travel and it would have been impossible, considering the point of entry of the cartridges, to achieve that travel within such a small arc of rotation to allow the gun to fire on top dead centre. These new guns, therefore, fired from the barrel at roughly the 7 o'clock position when viewed from the front. Not only that, the empty cases had to be physically pulled out of the chamber; this required that the bolt be fitted with an extractor to withdraw the cases and also demanded a simple and foolproof means of releasing them so that the loading, firing and extraction cycle could be repeated. As in the 'chamber-loading' guns, the bolt also had to support the base of the cartridge at the instant of firing. These fundamental elements of a new mechanism were covered in new patents, no. 47,631 of

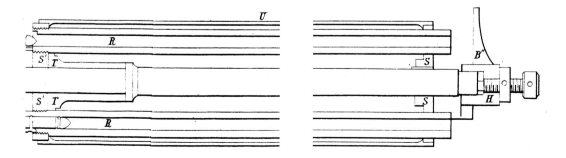

1865 (US) and no. 790 of 1865 (UK). The mechanism designed for the Model 1865 Gatling, with various refinements, provided the basic foundation for all future models.

This patent also incorporated two other features which did not appear on later guns and possibly did not appear on these guns in practice. Gatling recognized that one of the barrel and lock assemblies could become faulty through whatever cause. Such a fault could render the gun inoperable until repaired, so to overcome this he incorporated a blanking-off cap that could be clipped to the cartridge carrier associated with the faulty mechanism and which prevented a cartridge from dropping into place and being fed through the system with possibly serious damage resulting.

The second feature, one which would have been of benefit to the Ager and which was later adopted by Maxim – but seems never to have been actually used in practice by Gatling – was a cooling jacket surrounding the barrel cluster. This seems to be the first instance of a water jacket being proposed for cooling a barrel – the fact that it is patented suggests as much – but also seems never to have been acknowledged.

Early in 1865 Gatling transferred the manufacture of guns to the Cooper Fire Arms Manufacturing Company of Philadelphia, Pennsylvania, who, with their experience and reputation as firearms manufacturers were better equipped to produce the new guns; it was they who produced the last of the .58in-calibre rimfire guns and the first of the big 1in-calibre guns. In 1865, when the war was over, Major General John Love, acting as Gatling's agent, succeeded in initiating a series of official tests with a four-barrelled gun of .58in calibre at Washington Arsenal. These tests showed it capable of delivering 20 shots in 8 seconds, all striking the target and penetrating 11in of white pine boards at 300yd (*OM* §17: 18). A further test just over a year later with a 1in smoothbore gun firing canister shot containing 16 balls firing at a target 35.5ft long and 15ft high, made of 1in pine boards, showed that at a range of 250yd only 18 per cent hit the target and only 50 per cent of those penetrated (*OM* §17: 20). Shortly after, a test with a rifled 1in gun alongside a 24-pdr flank-defence howitzer was carried out. The Gatling, firing 'buck and ball' cartridges at the rate of about one per second, discharged in 1½ minutes around 1,600 projectiles; in the same time the 24-pdr only fired four rounds, giving, for canister 192, and for case shot 700, projectiles. The report also comments on the effect on morale of the Gatling 'in repelling an assault, as there is not a second of time for the assailants to advance between the discharges' (quoted in Wahl & Toppel 1965: 30).

After these trials, in 1866 – around which time the gun was altered to handle .50in centrefire cartridges as opposed to the .58in rimfire used previously – the US Government formally adopted the gun, and placed an order with Gatling for 50 each of the 1in- and .5in-calibre versions (Wahl & Toppel 1965: 31). With such a large contract, manufacture was once again transferred, this time to the Colt Patent Firearms Manufacturing Company. This order is confirmed by a note in the business diary of Major General William Buel Franklin, Vice President at Colt's: '27th September

OPPOSITE
A detail from the 1865 patent drawing showing the blanking-off cap for fitting over the cavity in the cartridge carrier if required. (Private collection)

Confirmation of Colt's entry into the Gatling story is provided by this nameplate from a Model 1865 Colt-manufactured Gatling, as in the first US Government contract. This nameplate has other points of interest – on the back it has part of a name, possibly of the brass founder who made it, and, intriguingly, the British War Office 'WD' mark. When acquired in the 1970s there were no screw holes in it; this, together with the fact that it is flat, shows that it was never fitted. (Private collection)

1866: Made contract with company for man'g [manufacturing] Gatling gun, one hundred'.[1]

Further tests resulted in two interesting comments. In 1867, a 'Report on certain defects in the Gatling gun' at Leavenworth Arsenal, Kansas, noted: 'the barrels were successively discharged before they had fairly cleared the front transverse bar of the gun frame, and that it was not the undermost barrel that fired'(*OM* §17: 21). A few days later, trials were carried out at the Watervliet Arsenal, New York to determine at what precise point in the revolution of the barrels, when they were turned both very slowly and rapidly, the cartridge was discharged. On slow turning, it was reported that the 'ball from the 1 inch gun cleared the bar by ³⁄₁₆th of an inch and that of the ½ inch gun by ⅛th of an inch; a more rapid motion causes the firing to take place at a lower point' (*OM* §17: 21). As a result of these tests, Brigadier General P.V. Hagner of the US Ordnance Department suggested the mechanism of the gun be changed so that each barrel fired when at its lowest position. Even so, in 1868, a report from Fort Leavenworth speaks of 'slugging of the balls on the front transverse bar' (*OM* §17: 21) but we are not told if this was an earlier gun or a later one in which the 'timing' had been adjusted. However, this fault does not appear to have been reported after this time so it is assumed it had been corrected.

THE MODELS OF 1869 AND 1871

In 1869 a further patent was granted in Britain (no. 3,341) but for some reason did not appear in the United States until two years later (no. 112,138). Possibly prompted by the significant improvements embodied in the 1869 patent, the British military authorities raised the subject again but, for some obscure reason, seemed still undecided over the merits of the Gatling or Montigny *mitrailleur* (as contemporaries called such weapons), which was favoured by at least one officer, Major Fosbery of the Bengal Staff Corps. However, in 1870, when the India Office enquired whether Major Fosbery should be ordered back to England, a reply was sent stating that 'Major Fosbery's services are not required in this country in connexion with the supply of a weapon which has been preferred to the one which he himself had recommended' (*DAS* §2873). Obviously by this time the superior merits

A composite image of details from UK patent no. 3,341 showing how the lock and plug engaged for lock withdrawal. On the inward end of the plug was a rotating collar (p¹) having a lug on its periphery with a forward-facing projection (a) with a groove. This groove corresponded with the lug (b¹) on the lock-head which engaged with the cam, giving the reciprocating motion to the lock as the barrel and lock assembly revolved. When each of the barrels was correctly aligned with a mark on the lock casing, its corresponding lock was engaged with the hook (a) on the plug and in line with the opening in the cascable. By rotating the plug to bring its lug in alignment with the cut-out in the cascable hole, the plug with the lock could be withdrawn. (Private collection)

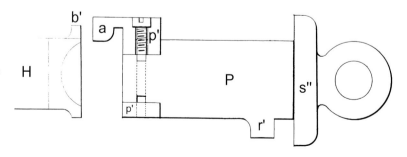

14

1   Private communication from Ed Hull; diary held in State Library, Hartford, Connecticut.

How the Gatling works

Figure 1 depicts the lock assembly of the earliest form of gun, using pre-loaded steel chambers, which were either loaded with powder and ball and fitted with a percussion cap at the rear and functioned as a cartridge, or had been bored through to allow them to contain a metallic cartridge. The lock carrier has been removed for clarity. It shows the instant of firing, where the lock and pre-loaded chamber are being pressed tightly against the mouth of the barrel by the lock being in contact with the projecting button (green) on the diaphragm (red) and the projection of the hammer (dark grey) has just passed the step on the circular cam (yellow) and has been driven forward by the spring (dark blue) just visible through the slot inside the lock casing. Continued revolution of the gun causes the lock to ride off the button (green), removing the pressure from the chamber, allowing it to drop out at the bottom.

    Figure 2 offers a three-dimensional representation of the lock assembly of a breech-loading gun using conventional self-contained metallic cartridge ammunition. It shows the sequence of feeding a cartridge into the chamber and retracting the hammer ready for release to fire it. For clarity the cams have been omitted. **Figure 3** depicts the same mechanism 'laid flat' to show how the various cams function as the assembly revolves clockwise – left to right – in causing the lock, acted upon by the green and red cams, to move forwards and backwards in feeding and withdrawing the cartridge and empty case, and how the hammer, acted upon by the blue cam, is moved backwards against the spring and released to fire the cartridge. (All images courtesy Rob Brassington)

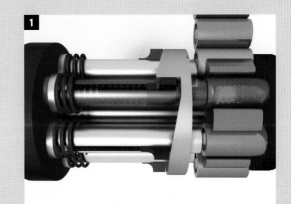

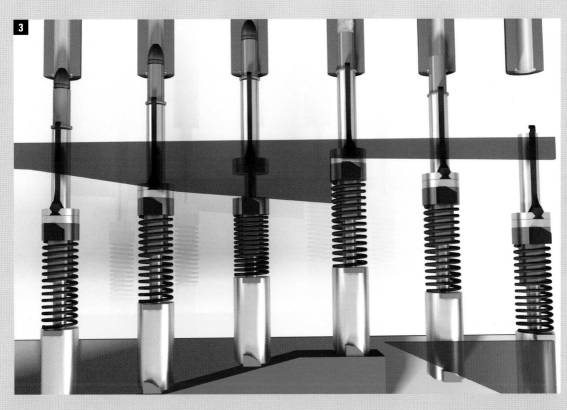

15

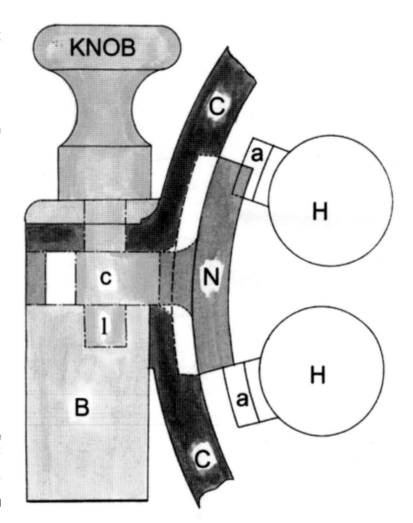

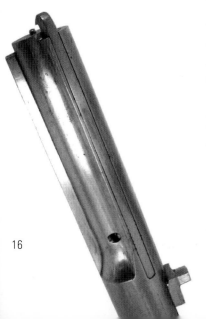

of the Gatling had been more fully appreciated. At this time also, in addition to considerations over calibre and ammunition Gatling licensed Sir W.G. Armstrong & Co. to make and vend Gatling guns in the United Kingdom of Great Britain, Ireland, the Channel Islands and the Isle of Man (Wahl & Toppel 1965: 41). This patent did not change the fundamental principles of the mechanical design but added some important refinements and changes in various features. These were: (1) the introduction of a moveable cocking cam; (2) a means of removing individual locks/bolts in case of malfunction; (3) the form of the locks; (4) more positive extractor engagement; (5) a means of automatically opening the feed box as soon as it was inserted into the gun. There was also a change from the use of bevel wheels to the use of worm-and-wheel to transfer hand-power to the mechanism.

The moveable cocking cam incorporated two features. It could simply be moved laterally so that it could be disengaged, allowing the gun to be demonstrated or used in drill training exercises without snapping the locks, which could obviously lead to damage. It could also be moved longitudinally to vary the degree to which the mainspring was compressed and therefore the force with which the hammer, or striker, struck the

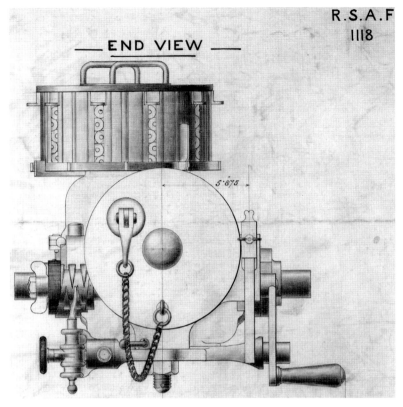

— END VIEW —

5·875

cartridge. While this is an obviously useful refinement, it has not been possible to determine how widely it may have been adopted although it was seemingly incorporated into the British-built guns of 1873 but without the projecting knob, judging from illustrations in various handbooks and the factory drawings. On the other hand, the ability to remove individual locks was of great importance; if one became non-functional through whatever cause, or a cartridge became jammed in a chamber, the gun would be rendered inoperable until repair could be undertaken. Gatling overcame this risk by providing a simple means of quickly removing a lock if necessary.

The changes in the form of the lock were twofold. First, the mainspring and hammer (striker/firing pin) were fully encased in the lock body, and secondly the lock body itself was in one piece and of a single diameter throughout with parts of the forward portion cut away as necessary. This allowed the lock to clear the trough in the cartridge carrier and feed the cartridge into the chamber; it also allowed the creation of an integral rib which rode in a slot in the cartridge carrier and prevented the lock from rotating on its own axis. The extractor was made so that when the cartridge was being fed, a slight play allowed the claw on the extractor to lift and ride over the cartridge rim. Conversely, when being withdrawn, the claw was securely pressed down onto the cartridge to prevent it from accidentally riding over the cartridge rim.

A major addition to the gun's attributes, an automatic traversing mechanism, received a British provisional patent in 1870, followed by full

THE GATLING RESTORED

.45in Royal Artillery Gatling

A restored standard British Army .45in Gatling gun, serial Number 41 and dated 1874, on the Royal Artillery field carriage, as opposed to the Royal Navy wheeled carriage known as a 'landing carriage'. The field carriage differed in various ways, most noticeably in having a straight 'axletree' – the iron shaft to which the wheels were fitted – as opposed to the naval version with a dip in its centre, and being fitted with trunnion bearings. It is awaiting the fitting of axletree boxes for the Broadwell drum magazines. (Private collection)

1. Front sight
2. Barrel cluster
3. Broadwell drum magazine
4. Lock casing
5. Lock withdrawing plug
6. Cascable plate
7. Tool box
8. Folding trail seat
9. Elevating handwheel
10. Elevating gearbox

11. Elevating screw
12. Brace
13. Auto-traversing gear
14. Traversing plate with trunnions
15. Trunnion bearing and capsquare
16. Cartridge carrier cover and magazine platform
17. Gun frame
18. Cover for headspace adjusting screw
19. Iron tyre
20. Drag shoe washer

21. Spokes (12 per wheel)
22. Felloes (six per wheel)
23. 'Madras' pattern hubs
24. Axletree
25. Crank handle
26. Rear sight
27. Iron trail side plates
28. Trail handle
29. Trail eye
30. Traversing lever

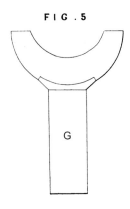

FIG.5

G

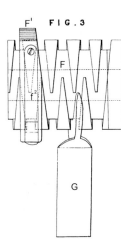

FIG.3

F'

F

f²

G

patent (no. 2,463) in 1871, followed by US patent no. 120,588, dated 7 November 1871. It was invented by George O. Kinne of Hartford, Connecticut. Since Colt's factory was in Hartford and was actively engaged in manufacturing the guns, it raises the question of whether Kinne was a Colt employee or an independent inventor. However, according to the US patent, Kinne is described as 'assignor to Colt's Patent Firearms Manufacturing Company'. It was an ingenious device, requiring the Gatling – or any similar gun – to be mounted on a separate mounting plate fitted to a pivot on the gun carriage.

Although actual construction details varied in practice, this allowed the gun to be moved laterally independently of the carriage. A refinement of this idea of Kinne's was covered in a UK patent (no. 380) by Lewis Broadwell, Gatling's agent in Vienna, in the same year and was certainly used on British-made guns. In this, the worm had a simple cone clutch device – the conical recesses in the ends of the worm are shown on this page – which was operated by a thumb nut threaded on the worm shaft, and is clearly shown on page 17. The alacrity with which this refinement was adopted is apparent from a commentary, published in *The Times* on 6 October 1873 and concerning the Third Anglo-Ashanti War of 1873–74:

> The gun is fitted with an arrangement by which a traversing motion may be given to the barrels while the firing continues. It is obvious that it would be absurd constantly to fire a Gatling gun in one direction. A few men immediately in front would be perforated, while those on the flanks would escape. But the traversing arrangement enables us to 'waterpot' the enemy with a leaden rain.

Around the same time, a Mr H. Bigg put forward a proposal to improve the lateral spreading of shots by 'hinging together three sets of Gatling barrels together at their bases without interfering with their rotary action, and then by a simple and easily regulated mechanism spreading laterally the two outer series of barrels while the centre remains stationary' (*DAS* §3227). It sounds excessively complicated and the President of the Committee to which this proposal was made recommended that no encouragement was to be given to Mr Bigg!

Broadwell's UK patent no. 380 also covered the use of a wrought-iron carriage in place of the traditional timber variety; this also incorporated a folding shield to protect the gunners while in action. The granting of a patent for this suggests it was the first carriage of its kind and within a few years, iron gun carriages had become more or less standard practice. By 1870, however, it would seem that the first guns for the British War Department were being manufactured by Armstrong's, who were additionally asked to submit a design for an iron field carriage. It would appear that this, after various small changes to reduce weight, was adopted and differed from Broadwell's design quite markedly in having plain iron-plate sides with round bolts acting as transoms (cross bracing or spacers) and which, almost beneath the breech of the gun, commenced tapering towards a very narrow trail piece.

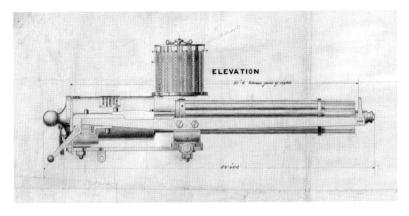

ELEVATION

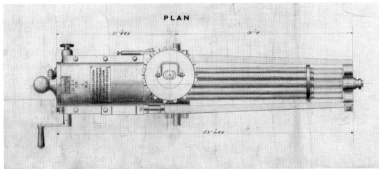

PLAN

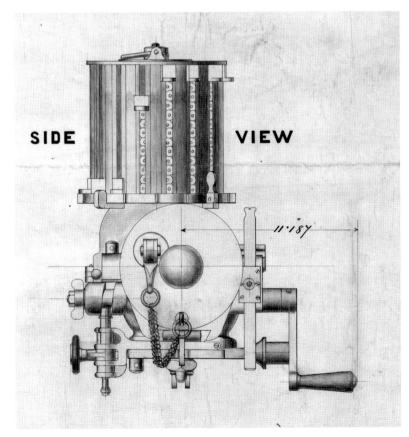

SIDE VIEW

Feed boxes and magazines

Gatling's first patent simply states that the pre-loaded chambers 'are placed in the hopper or reservoir', which would appear to mean they are manually placed in the hopper since there is no mention in the patent of any form of magazine. This hopper is clearly visible on the gun shown on page 10. By the time of the 1865 patent, however, specific reference is made to a 'cartridge-box into which the cartridges are packed for transportation and out of which they are fed by their own gravity, one by one, into the cavities of the carrier as it revolves beneath them'. On these guns, the feed hopper has been replaced by an angled 'socket' on the hinged action cover plate into which the 'cartridge box' or 'feed box' – a magazine in modern terms – was inserted.

In 1870 a magazine with greater capacity than the linear magazines was patented by Lewis Wells Broadwell. Becoming known as the 'Broadwell Drum', it is a feature seen on many Gatlings illustrated in the 1870s and was the only type used in British service. It was described by Broadwell in his US patent no. 110,338 of 1870 as 'a revolving feeding cylinder ... which is composed of a tube having arranged radially around it feeding chambers tapering inward, the whole being suitably braced top and bottom ...'. Handling the drum was made easy by having a carrying handle on top. As the gun was operated, cartridges were then fed under gravity, assisted by the sliding weight. As far as British service was concerned there were two sizes of Broadwell drum magazine to match the cartridges in use – in this case the .45in and

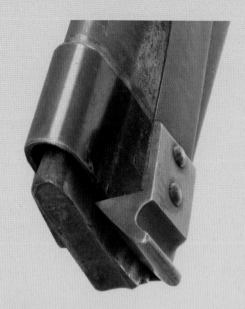

ABOVE The right-hand bottom portion of a .45-70 feed box showing the cartridge follower emerging after the last cartridge has been removed. (Courtesy of Joss Grandeau collection; photograph by David Alderson)

.65in. The .45in drum had 16 columns of 15 cartridges, i.e. a capacity of 240, and weighed 50lb when full (Admiralty 1877: 3); the .65in drum had ten columns of five cartridges, i.e. a total capacity of 50, and weighed 46.4lb when full (*LoC* §3325).

Gatling's US patent drawings of 1871, which mirror the UK patent of 1869, show his retention of a curved box-magazine system fitted at an angle on the left-hand side of the gun, although the UK patent has no indication that the magazine box is curved. Admittedly, his 1869 patent could not incorporate a feature of a patent which was yet to appear, but his 1871 US patent could have, so it may be that Gatling was working out some form of patent licensing agreement with Broadwell. The drum magazine certainly featured in Gatling's US patent no. 125,563 of 1872.

Probably the other most significant feed/magazine systems were the Bruce feed and the Accles drum. The Bruce feed was patented by Lucien F. Bruce of Springfield, Massachusetts, in 1881 (US patent no. 247,158). It was an attempt to provide an effective gravity-feed system which could be loaded simply and more quickly than those used up to that time. It may be that the Gatling Gun Co. very quickly bought these patent rights because the identical UK patent – no. 4,211, granted nine days later – is in the company's name.

All the feed devices so far used had relied on gravity to carry the cartridges into the gun. In contrast, the system patented by James G. Accles in 1881 (UK patent no. 5,436) and 1883 (US patent no. 290,622) was 'positive' in that the cartridges were mechanically fed into the gun by the operation of the gun mechanism itself. The magazine looked like a square-cornered bronze doughnut with a

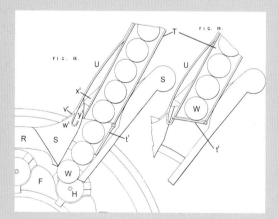

ABOVE The feed box as shown in UK patent no. 3,341 of 1869. The cover (R) of the carrier block (F) had a hopper (S) formed on its left-hand end into which the feed box (T) was inserted. As the box was pushed downwards, an extension (v^1) of the spring latch (U) encountered an incline (w^1) on the hopper (S). As the feed box was pushed further, this incline forced the latch (U) outwards, disengaging its tip from the flap (t^1), allowing the flap to fall open and release the cartridges (W) into the carrier (F) in front of the locks (H). At this point, a projection (X^1) on the feed box encountered a projection (y^1) inside the hopper and stopped the feed box from being inserted further. (Private collection)

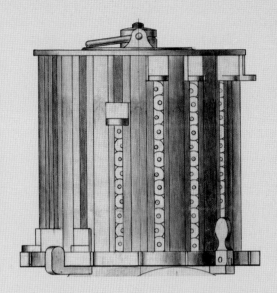

carrying handle and held 104 of the .45-70 cartridges. Filling the drum by hand through the small opening was time-consuming and a loading device was patented by L.F. Bruce (UK patent no. 6,009 of 1886). Although seemingly robust, the drums were easily damaged in the rigours of military service so they were not wholly successful. However, their great advantage of positive feed enabled guns fitted with them to operate effectively at more severe inclinations than was practical with the gravity-feed systems.

Other 'positive' feed systems were developed towards the end of the 19th century – a metallic strip-feed device, similar to that used in Hotchkiss machine guns, by Accles in 1891 (UK patent no. 17,885 of 1891); another strip feed by Broderick and Vankeirsbilck (UK patent no. 504,516 of 1893), and a belt feed by Gatling himself

(UK patent no. 504,831 of 1893). It seems unlikely that any of these systems were adopted, since in 1898 the US Government fitted all of its Model 1883 Gatlings with another device patented by Bruce in 1886 (possibly UK patent no. 7,659), which made the standard Bruce feed 'more positive', and at the same time rendered the Accles drum obsolete in military service. However, another device patented by Bruce (UK patent no. 2,228 of 1890) also incorporated a positive-feed system and the correspondence of patent dates suggests this was featured in the Model 1890 gun (see page 27).

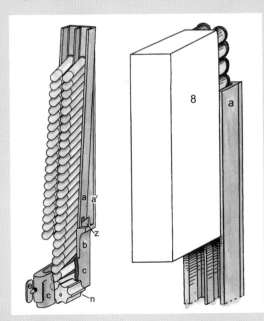

LEFT Details of the Bruce feed, adapted from the drawing for US patent no. 247,158 of 1881. It consisted of a double-row of vertical channels (a) – referred to as 'conductors' in the patent – in which the cartridges were held by their heads. This was pivoted at the top of a column (a^1) extending upwards from a foot (c) which was used to fix it to the feed hopper on the top of the breech casing by means of the clamping screw (e). At the lower end of this column, immediately above the opening to the feed hopper, a single cartridge channel was formed in the portion (b) and over which each of the channels on the pivoted portion could be swung in turn. At the bottom of the column (a^1) was an inclined plane or wedge (z) on each side. Each wedge protruded into a channel and a column of cartridges rested on it. When one column was emptied, the weight of the cartridges in the second channel on this inclined plane caused the double-row of vertical channels (a) to be swung on its pivot so that the second column of cartridges was now in line with the single channel at the bottom and could be fed into the gun. Before entering the gun, a fluted roller (n) straightened the cartridges which, being nose-heavy, tended to tilt downwards. Filling the 'magazine' was straightforward. The cartridges were packed in card boxes (8) in two rows with spacing to match the spacing of the channels in the feed column (a). When the lid of the box was removed, the heads of the cartridges were exposed for a sufficient length to allow them to be slid into the feed channels as the cartridge box was moved downwards. When all the cartridges were inserted, the box was simply pulled forward, leaving the cartridges in place. A later modification added an upright extension of the column (a^1), with a fence at one edge to aid fast alignment of the cartridge box. (Private collection)

THE MODELS OF 1874

Although often referred to as the Model 1874, these guns incorporated the main feature of US patent no. 125,563 (1872), which was a very much smaller lock (see illustrations below). In addition, dovetail-shaped tenons or ribs (in later guns these were 'T'-shaped) on the bottom of the locks fitting in matching-shaped slots in the lock carrier meant that the locks did not have to be fully enclosed to keep them in place, i.e. they could not fall out during rotation. The outer portion of most of the lock carrier could therefore be eliminated and this, in conjunction with the much smaller bolts, enabled a much shorter and lighter lock casing to be used. In their excellent book Wahl and Toppel also state that this patent introduced the headspace-adjusting screw on the front cross-bar of the frame. When used, the barrels heated up, of course, and in doing so expanded lengthways; this could cause a tightening of the action. A screw, passing through the cross-bar, bore on the main shaft and when the barrels became heated, unscrewing this screw slightly, allowed the expansion to be taken care of and eliminated any tightness. In fact, however, this facility was covered in Gatling's first patent of 1862.

The Model 1874 gun came in two distinct configurations, one having 32in 'musket length' barrels and the other, the so-called 'camel gun', with 18in barrels. Although no such Gatling-equipped camel corps has ever been heard of, it was certainly an intriguing and eye-catching marketing device, and it has been suggested to have its origins with a Colonel Maxwell of the Royal Artillery, Superintendent of the Cossipore Gun Foundry in India, who recounted to an audience at Woolwich the story of an Afghan chief who attacked the Persians with an army mounted on camels, hidden in the middle of which were many with a swivel gun attached to the saddle (Rogers 1875: 427–28). Perhaps in view of the fanciful nature of this name, the shortened versions later became known as 'bulldogs'. Apart from the suggested camel mounting, this gun could be supplied with a tripod in place of – or in addition to – a 'cavalry cart', which was a two-wheeled carriage having a small flat bed onto which the cradle of the gun was fitted directly. This was the first time a tripod had

These details of the locks from the US patent no. 112,138 of 1871 (above) and no. 125,563 of 1872 (below) show just how much shorter the 1872 locks were. The 1872 locks were also smaller in diameter owing to the lack of the projecting cocking lug on the striker. (Private collection)

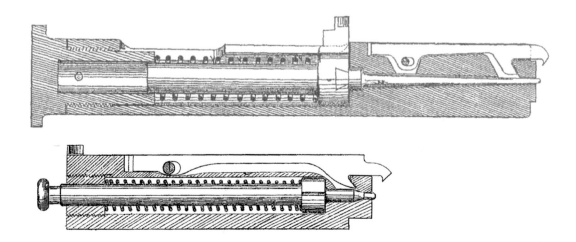

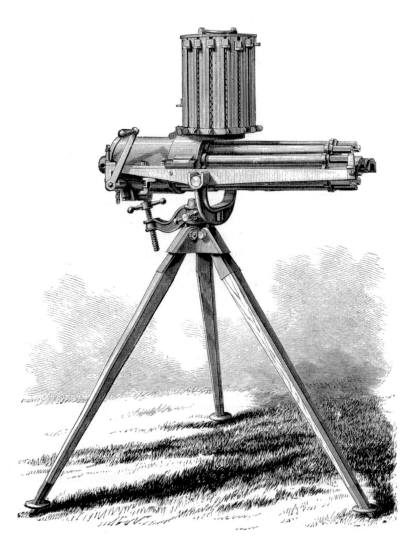

A Model 1874 'camel gun' on a tripod mount. From Norton 1880, facing p. 269. (Private collection)

been used, made possible by the much-shortened and lighter gun, and were to feature with subsequent models also. This patent also includes an automatic traversing arrangement which is basically identical in principle to that patented by Kinne in 1870/71 and assigned to Colt's. How such a patent was granted to Gatling in the face of an existing one-year-old patent is puzzling!

THE MODEL 1877 'BULLDOG' GATLINGS AND AFTER

Following the 1872 patent and the guns developed from it there were no really fundamental changes to the gun's basic mechanism, although a confusing variety of 'models' appeared which reflected changes that began to appear with the 'camel gun' – although by this time the short guns had become the 'bulldogs'. There were variations on the number of barrels and their lengths; whether they were encased or not; the types of mounting, which tended to be either a wheeled carriage of some form or a tripod;

and the ammunition feed system used. For instance, some Model 1874 guns made for the US Navy had their barrels encased in a bronze sleeve, though it is unclear whether this was an attempt to provide a cooling system, as outlined in the patent of 1865 (see page 12), or to protect barrels from the elements.

It was also at this time that another, very distinctive feature began to appear – the mounting of the crankshaft directly on the main shaft which projected through the cascable plate. This feature does not appear to be the subject of any patent, though it was shown in Gatling's patent of 1893. The elimination of the drive gears meant much higher rates of fire could be achieved – in 1880 it was being reported that they could fire over 1,000 rounds per minute, a phenomenal rate for the period, especially when considering they relied on gravity feed and that the Maxim gun could only achieve around 400–600 per minute.

The Model 1883 Gatling, though, perhaps typifies the combined features then available. The barrels were encased in a bronze jacket; the main shaft passed through the cascable button but the gearing was retained so the handle could be fitted on the side for geared drive, or on the end of the main shaft for direct drive. Obviously there must have been some simple means of disconnecting the gears because with a worm gear, only the worm can be the prime mover – and it prevented the worm wheel from being rotated directly. In direct drive, this model could supposedly achieve 1,500 rounds per minute! Because of this, the components were made stronger and there was a reversion to the long lock, or bolt, seen in the 1869 and 1871 versions. In addition, these guns, at that sort of rate, certainly needed to ensure ammunition supply was maintained; this could not be done by gravity alone and so the Accles positive feed was used.

Despite the enhanced performance of the Model 1883 guns, the extra cost of encasing the barrels in bronze and manufacturing the complex Accles feed drum, plus the slowness of reloading the drum, led to a reversion to the more orthodox designs typified by the Model 1890. Wahl and Toppel comment that the improvement in this model incorporated a device known as the 'Murphy stop', a cocking switch which allowed the cocking cam to be disengaged so the gun would not fire during rotation. It was a variation of the device covered in the 1869 British and the 1871 US patents but with the control knob forming the cascable 'button' and which, having to be pulled out as well as rotated, gave a more positive action, and was retained on subsequent models.

Apart from changes in ammunition (see page 31), the Model 1890 formed the basis of the Model 1895, Model 1900 and Model 1903, the last to be used by the US forces since by this time the Gatling gun was finally being eclipsed by the fully automatic weapons of Maxim and Browning.

LEFT A Model 1890 in .45in calibre (presumably the standard .45-70 Government cartridge), restored and with new tripod and yoke. It would appear to be fitted with a simple feed box but the patent date on the gun (11 February 1890) corresponds with that of a further Bruce UK patent for a positive-feed device. (Courtesy James D. Julia, Inc. (Auctions) via Steve Fjestad, Blue Book Publications)

RIGHT According to the inscription on the casing, this is a Model 1900. It appears to be fitted with the Bruce feed system as modified in 1886, and is in .30in calibre, for the .30-40 Krag cartridge – a rare survival, since in 1906 guns were altered to accept the new .30-06 cartridge. The turntable is dated 1883 and the inscription shows US Navy purchase, so it may be that the tripod is not original to this gun. It was the earlier version of this gun, fitted on field carriages, that featured in the Spanish–American War. (Courtesy James D. Julia, Inc. (Auctions) via Steve Fjestad, Blue Book Publications)

Gatling tools

Details of these, like the objects themselves, are very scarce. Most of the information available is to be found in various surviving handbooks, rarities in themselves, for the American and British guns. In addition there are some workshop drawings of the tools prepared at Britain's Royal Small Arms Factory (RSAF), not all of which can be shown here.

In the US handbook for the .30in-calibre Gatling gun, for instance, there are ten various tools listed and illustrated (Ordnance Department 1917: 29), but the nature of the printing and the small size of the image do not lend themselves to high-definition reproduction. In addition, many are similar to ordinary tools and may not be distinguishable as Gatling tools unless they have Ordnance codes or other markings. One – the cascable-plate wrench shown on this page – is unusual, both in shape and the fact that it is made of bronze. As far as British service is concerned, the handbooks for naval (Admiralty 1877) and land service (War Office 1880) guns list 14 tools, none of which is illustrated, and very few appear to survive. Similarly, a complete set of drawings of them has not been found.

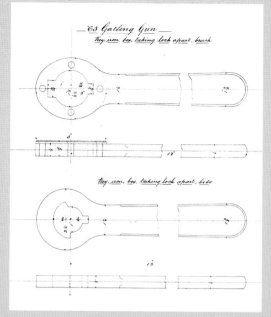

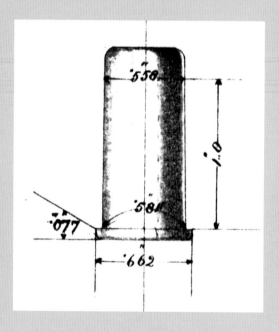

ABOVE RSAF drawing no. 132 showing the two wrenches, or 'keys', used for removing the head of the lock assembly of the .65in gun so that it could be dismantled. Each matched the profile of the lock body where it was applied. Not dated, but part of a series of drawings prepared in 1875–76. (Courtesy Trustees of Royal Armouries; author's own photograph reproduced by kind permission of the Royal Armouries, RSAF 132)

LEFT Drawing of the cartridge gauge for .45in Gatling and Gardner guns as shown in RSAF drawing no. 827, dated 1882. (Courtesy Trustees of Royal Armouries; author's own photograph reproduced by kind permission of the Royal Armouries, RSAF 827)

BELOW The cascable-plate wrench, listed as item no. 131 in the US handbook for the .30in-calibre Gatling gun (Ordnance Department 1917, plate IV). (Private collection)

USE
The Gatling at war

The Gatling gun was gradually adopted by many nations other than the United States and saw service in various conflicts across the globe. Yet curiously, despite the iconic status it has achieved, its actual use was not as extensive as one might imagine. However, assessing the distribution and deployment of the gun outside of the United States is not always easy, largely on account of a tendency, both in official and public accounts, to describe any multifiring or multibarrelled weapon under the generic term *mitrailleur*. This may stem from the comments made by Major Fosbery of the Bengal Staff Corps in 1869: 'Mitrailleur, the term I have adopted ... perhaps best of all expresses what is intended ... and to avoid confusion, I shall apply it to these inventions indiscriminately, whether or not in my opinion all are equally deserving of the title' (Fosbery 1869: 540). However, far from preventing confusion, Captain E. Rogers in 1876 rightly noted it to be a 'term which, by the way, is apt to mislead' (Rogers 1875: 420).

IN US SERVICE

The American Civil War
One might imagine that, as an American invention, conceived in a desire to mitigate mortality soon after the human effects of the Civil War became apparent – and having been shown to work – the Gatling would be immediately adopted for use by the Union forces in that conflict. However, from what limited evidence is available it would seem the Gatling saw little, if any, combat service in the Civil War. We are told that 'a weapon with 25 barrels, resembling the mitrailleur' (Fletcher 1872: 34) was

29

Dr Josephus Requa's volley gun, .52in calibre, built by William Billinghurst of Rochester, New York. (US National Park Service, Springfield Armory National Historic Site Photograph. Acc. No. SPAR 5611)

employed during the Union attack on Fort Wagner in 1863, but this was probably a Billinghurst–Requa volley gun, sometimes known as the 'covered bridge' gun because, although there was some ability to adjust the barrels to give a 'spread', it still provided a relatively narrow field of fire ideal for use within the confined space of a covered, or even open, bridge.

In fact, the only evidence for the use of Gatlings in the field seem to concern those purchased by the Union's Major General Benjamin Butler at his own expense. They were employed during the Bermuda Hundred campaign, a precursor to battle at Petersburg, but it has been suggested they were only set up, test-fired and placed in Butler's fortified position for show rather than actual use.[2] On the other hand, Gatling himself states they were 'used effectively in repelling Rebel attacks upon the Union Forces, under command of General Butler, near Richmond, Virginia' (Gatling 1870: 509). Similarly, it is suggested that Rear Admiral D.D. Porter also purchased some for the Mississippi River Squadron, but no evidence has been discovered to indicate they were actually used.

Some steel 'loading chambers' found by collectors in recent times at sites of Civil War battles has led to some speculation that these are from Gatling guns. However, the great similarity between the chambers used on the Ager gun and those of the Gatling does not help in finding an unequivocal answer to this question. It was later noted that

> It is in the US that the utility of the Gatling has been appreciated. Two natures of the weapon issued to American navy, one with long and one with short barrels. Pivot sockets are fixed in convenient positions on the rails and in the tops of large vessels ... When used ashore, 13 men are assigned to serve it ... (Rogers 1875: 425)

A chamber for the Ager gun, very similar to those used with the first Gatlings of 1862. (US National Park Service, Springfield Armory National Historic Site Photograph)

Yet by the time this was written, the utility of the Gatling had already been widely appreciated and put to use by a number of other countries.

2   Personal communication from the late Tom Stelma, Montgomery, Texas.

US Gatling ammunition

It has already been mentioned that the first Gatling used a pre-loaded steel or iron chamber fitted with an external percussion cap. Few, if any, of these appear to have survived but they would not have been very different from those used with the Ager. The first self-contained ammunition to be used was the .58in rimfire cartridge, made possible in the first guns by simply having these chambers bored all the way through, allowing a cartridge to be inserted from the rear. In the United States, Gatlings were made to handle the same cartridge as the military rifles of the time. So when, in 1865, the gun was redesigned to handle self-contained metallic cartridges, these were first, the .58in rimfire and then the .58in centrefire. This was followed by the .50in infantry cartridge. Of course the 1in calibre guns did not correspond with any military rifle!

The so-called Model 1874 Naval Gatling used the .50in cartridge of the Remington rifle (Marvin 1875: 16). However, with the adoption of the .45-70 cartridge for military rifles in 1873, Gatlings were made to chamber the same cartridge. Then, beginning in 1895, a series of relatively rapid changes occurred. The Model 1895 and Model 1900 were chambered to use the .30-40 cartridge used by the Krag-Jørgensen rifle, the United States' first bolt-action magazine rifle using smokeless powder. The Gatling Model 1903 was chambered for the cartridge adopted for the new Model 1903 rifle, often referred to as the .30-03; in contrast with the .30-40 Krag, this was a rimless cartridge. There was another fairly quick change to the ammunition in 1906 with the adoption of the *spitzer* – pointed – bullet. At this time, all Gatlings in US Government service – Model 1895, Model 1900 and Model 1903 – were altered to accept this new .30-06 cartridge.

ABOVE US cartridges through the later 19th and into the early 20th century. Left: .45-70 Government; centre: .30-40 Krag (both US National Park Service, Springfield Armory National Historic Site Photograph); right: .30-06, identical to the .30-03 cartridge except for the bullet shape, which made it also slightly longer (Private collection).

ABOVE US .58in cartridges. Left: rimfire (1862); right: Berdan-primed centrefire (1865). (US National Park Service, Springfield Armory National Historic Site Photograph)

ABOVE Left (private collection): A short, inside-primed centrefire 1in cartridge with solid-lead bullet, 1865; what might appear at first sight as a rimfire cartridge is, in fact, centrefire using the Benet internal primer held in place by two crimps, a giveaway feature of this type of cartridge, which preceded the Berdan type. Centre (US National Park Service, Springfield Armory National Historic Site Photograph): A long, Berdan-primed centrefire 1in cartridge. Right (private collection): A long, 'canister' 1in cartridge with both bullet and large buckshot. From Norton 1880, facing p. 277.

After 1865

After the Civil War, US forces used Gatlings alongside artillery in the arming of forts on the frontiers against attacks by Native Americans, although there were some 'domestic situations' in which they found a place. Some were apparently stationed in Salt Lake City in the event of trouble in that area (Fletcher 1872: 40), though there is no apparent record of them being used. There is also a little known incident where they were prepared for action, and may indeed have been used – the so-called 'Battle of Liberty Place' in New Orleans on 14 September 1874 (see Landry 1955). In the years of reconstruction which followed the Civil War there were instances of violence directed against freed blacks and Republican officials. Despite his country having undergone tremendous loss of life in fighting for the freedom of African Americans, President Ulysses S. Grant adopted the attitude of letting matters take their course in the Southern states, rather than to risk involving the US Government in a 'race war', and he did little to curb white militancy. A vigilante group, the 'White League', created in Louisiana in the spring and summer of 1874, had gathered 14,000 members, mostly Confederate veterans, within a few months. They were dedicated to a 'white man's government' and the suppression of 'the insolent and barbarous African'. Grant's policy of *laissez faire* encouraged 3,500 armed members of the White League to assemble in New Orleans on 14 September 1874, and demand that the 'carpetbagger' Republican Governor of Louisiana, William Pitt Kellogg, resign.

Opposing them were 3,600 policemen and African-American militia troops under the command of ex-Confederate Major General James Longstreet, who had ordered eight Gatlings from Colt's in 1871. He now formed a battle line containing two Gatling guns and a battery of artillery to guard the Customs House in which the governor and other Republican officials had taken refuge. The White League charged the line, captured Longstreet, and pushed his men to the river, where they either surrendered or fled. The attackers occupied the city hall, statehouse and arsenal. Total

The opening of the new National Rifle Association shooting range at Creedmoor, New York, on Saturday 21 June 1873. Perhaps the American outlook on the Gatling is best summarized by the fact that latest model, with Broadwell iron carriage and drum magazine, was used to fire the first shots. It is reported as being of .42in calibre and at a range of 200yd, every shot of the 400 fired hit the target. Unfortunately, the size of target is not reported, though – according to New York's *Daily Graphic* of 26 June 1873 – 'The rich dresses of officers and privates, and the fine scenery in the neighbourhood, rendered the scene attractive and inspiring'! *Daily Graphic*, 26 June 1873, p. 8. (Private collection)

casualties in the one-hour fight that has become known as the Battle of Liberty Place were 38 killed and 79 wounded. Whether the Gatlings actually fired is not recorded, though had they done so, the slaughter would probably have been extreme and would have made bold headlines. It was a very short victory – within three days Grant had ordered federal troops to New Orleans and on their arrival, the White Leaguers withdrew; Kellogg was reinstated as governor and Longstreet was released.

Only four instances have been found which record the actual use of Gatlings in earnest by US forces prior to the Spanish–American War of 1898 and in each case they were employed in engagements with Native Americans, in the field rather than from a fort. In the relentless quest for land – and possibly other treasure – with a total disregard for any birthrights of the Native Americans who happened to be in the way of 'progress', it was inevitable that sooner or later, trouble would erupt. But even in these battles, the use of Gatlings was very limited and there appear to be few direct observations on their use and effectiveness.

The Red River War

The first of these engagements was in the Red River War in West Texas in 1874. On 27 July, Colonel Nelson Miles was ordered to assemble an expedition at Fort Dodge in Kansas and move south of the Arkansas River to campaign against the Native Americans, mainly Cheyenne, holding back from entering the designated reservations. Part of this expedition comprised an artillery detachment of 21 men of the 5th Infantry under

A US Broadwell iron carriage of *c.*1871. From Norton 1880, facing p. 285. (Private collection)

F.L. SEITZ fecit

Lieutenant Pope and consisting of a 3in, 10-pdr, Parrott rifle and two .50in-calibre Gatlings. The first fighting took place on the plains of the Griffin Hills and it was here that Gatling guns were first put into action.

In one account (Wahl & Toppel 1966: 80) we are told that at 4am on 30 August an advance scouting party led by Lieutenant Baldwin followed a trail that led between bluffs and was ambushed by around 250 Native Americans who charged down from both sides. In another version, Baldwin claimed it was 200 Indians, while a third source, which is part of the official report by Colonel Miles, gives the number as being between 75 and 100 (Cruse 2008: 54). But regardless of the number of Native Americans, Pope quickly brought up his Gatlings and put up a barrage which repelled the attackers, who were then pursued by cavalry. This was obviously not a major engagement from the military point of view, though it did, perhaps, demonstrate under combat conditions the deterrent value of the Gatling.

Some confusion also exists in certain quarters about the second incident involving Gatling guns which also occurred in the Red River campaign. Captain Rogers, writing in 1875 in London, claimed that 'Major Price, of the 8th United States Cavalry, was attacked by 600 or 700 Indians, and he used his Gatlings with such excellent effect as to quite demoralize and drive off his savage assailants' (Rogers 1875: 427). The problem is that Price did not have any Gatling guns as part of his force; Rogers had obviously been misinformed. The second employment of the Gatling actually occurred on 6 April 1875, at the Cheyenne Agency in Indian Territory where a Cheyenne

Red River, 30 August 1876 (opposite)

The first indisputable use of the Gatling in combat in America took place when Lieutenant Baldwin's advance scouting party, following a trail leading between bluffs in the early hours of the morning, was ambushed by a party of Cheyenne warriors. The main body of Colonel Nelson Miles' expeditionary force consisted of a Gatling detachment of the 5th Infantry under Lieutenant Pope. While the American soldiers in their mainly dark uniforms set against the dark scrubland at the bottom of the slopes and below the horizon would have been difficult for the Cheyenne to see in detail, a faint glow of dawn in the east may have been sufficient to silhouette the Cheyenne and their horses on the small hill. Pope brought his two Gatlings to the front and put them into action, moving them as needed to keep up a fire on the Indians.

Here, we have shown the Model 1874 Gatling with straight 'stick' type magazines, each holding probably 40 of the .50in-calibre cartridges. During rapid fire, these would be emptied quickly and need almost continual replacement by a man or men detailed to the task. By the time of this action, most Native Americans had become familiar with a variety of firearms that were encountered on the frontiers in the hands of either settlers or soldiers and which they had acquired by various means. Some even had repeating firearms such as the Henry, or the more modern Winchester of 1866, or even the Spencer carbine or rifle. But the Gatling gun's performance as a repeating firearm was in a whole new league. Fired at full tilt the sound would have been a continuous crackle, not the individual spaced shots from a repeating rifle, and a flame would pour from the muzzle almost like a jet. In the darkness of an early morning, hearing and seeing such a weapon which spewed forth lead, flame, noise and smoke for the first time must have been verging on the supernatural. However the Gatlings were perceived, the barrage they put up was sufficient to cause the Cheyenne to break off their attack and flee.

prisoner was being fitted with shackles prior to being transported to prison at Fort Marion in Florida. In attempting to escape he was shot and killed by troopers of the 5th Infantry. This panicked the nearby Cheyenne camp and the villagers took refuge behind a hill on the south bank of the North Fork of Canadian River. Here they were able to recover a buried cache of arms and ammunition. Lieutenant Colonel Thomas Neill ordered a Gatling gun to be brought up and fired into the Cheyenne position to flush them out. It obviously worked because next morning Neill discovered they had fled to the north-west and pursuit of them led to the last of the battles against the Cheyenne at Sappa Creek in Kansas. The US Army attacked a small band of Southern Cheyenne fleeing north. Some claim it to be a massacre and that of the 27 Indians it is said were killed, a significant number were women and children. This engagement finally subdued the Cheyenne and they were herded onto their reservation.

The Nez Perce War

The third use of the Gatlings was also a result of this relentless push westwards and in this instance it was the peaceable Nez Perce who were the victims. It was they, in the winter of 1805–06, who had sheltered and cared for the members and horses of the Lewis and Clark Expedition, saving the explorers from starvation and certain death and nursing them back to health. In the early 1850s, settlers had begun to encroach on the homelands of the Nez Perce so a treaty with the government in 1855 recognized the just rights of the *Nee-Me-Poo* – the 'real people' in Nez Perce language – to their homelands and 'gave' the Nez Perce a tract of land about 250 miles long and 150 miles wide that covered parts of Washington, Idaho and Oregon territories at their junction with Montana and incorporated much of the Nez Perce's traditional mountain, rivers, trails and hunting grounds.

In 1860 gold was discovered in the valleys of the Snake and Clearwater Rivers and suddenly the region was awash with prospectors, miners and speculators and in their wake, more settlers and merchants. Despite the huge encroachments on their land, the Nez Perce protested peacefully. They could claim that they had honoured their treaty with the government and had never killed a 'white man'. The same could not be claimed by the settlers, or the government. In 1863, the Nez Perce reservation was reduced by almost 90 per cent to allow this new greed to be exercised, lawfully if not morally. Old Chief Joseph refused to sign the new treaty. Further erosion of lands took place as more space was opened up to settlers and by 1877 the situation had become intolerable to the Nez Perce and the last major Indian War began.

The Gatling gun made its first appearance of the campaign at the battle of the Clearwater. Here, under the command of Major General O.O. Howard, the Army occupied a high plateau overlooking the river and the

Oliver Otis Howard (8 November 1830–26 October 1909) was a Union general in the Civil War. As a brigade commander in the Army of the Potomac, Howard lost his right arm while leading his men against Confederate forces at Fair Oaks in June 1862, and for which action he later gained the Congressional Medal of Honor. He came to be known as the 'Christian general' as he based many policy decisions on his deep religious outlook; he was given charge of the Freedmen's Bureau in mid-1865, with the mission of integrating freed slaves into Southern society and, as a means of giving higher-education opportunities to freedmen, helped found Howard University in Washington, DC. (Library of Congress)

camp of the Nez Perce. Howard ordered his artillery to open fire on the camp but the guns could not be depressed sufficiently so all the shells did was to frighten the women and children and anger the warriors. The Nez Perce had detected the presence of the Army and had organized themselves into three groups: one to guard the camp, a second to drive the livestock and horses to safety, and the third to move to the ridgeline of the plateau to prevent the troops from advancing. Despite Howard's force of 400 greatly outnumbering the small Nez Perce contingent facing them, the Army contingent was surrounded and pinned down. The Nez Perce controlled all the surrounding land and the water supplies.

As the Army perimeter shrank under the attack of the Nez Perce, a howitzer and two Gatlings left stranded in no man's land were quickly recovered by the Army. At some stage it was noticed that Chief Joseph was present on the ridge; it then became a target for the artillery and the Gatlings, which raked the ridge with fire as the Nez Perce sank deeper into their sheltered positions. An Army relief column of pack horses loaded with supplies, escorted by a troop of cavalry, appeared in the distance. As the soldiers extended their flank to protect the mule train, they also placed themselves in position to attack the flank of the Nez Perce and dislodge

The Dead Mule Trail in Clearwater County, Idaho, shown here in a sketch by an Army officer during the Nez Perce War, was a treacherous path across the mountains and typical of many such passes. The use of any form of wheeled transport, including Gatling and other gun carriages, was impossible, unless they could be dismantled for carriage by pack animals, and the time lost in dismantling and packing made close pursuit a forlorn and dangerous undertaking. (Library of Congress)

them. As the Nez Perce withdrew down the hill, the Gatlings were once again put into action and, though they did little harm, served to encourage the retreat (Carson 2011: 108).

The Army had been held long enough where the Nez Perce wanted them to allow their women and children to be moved to safety, and they quickly vanished into the Clearwater Canyon and through the Kamiah Valley. Once through, the Nez Perce crossed the river and positioned themselves on the high ground from where they fired on the pursuing cavalry, forcing them to withdraw. Two days later the Army were still no further forward, unable to cross the river without serious casualties, and the soldiers spent their time getting into the best fighting positions they could while under constant fire, occasionally replying using the Gatlings to sweep the high ground. By the morning of 5 October, both sides were exhausted; winter would soon be upon them and the Nez Perce had no supply lines to come to their aid. It was at this point that Chief Joseph spoke his famous

words to his followers: 'Hear me, my chiefs. I am tired; my heart is sick and sad. From where the sun now stands I will fight no more forever' (quoted in Carson 2011: 234). He then went and handed his rifle to Colonel Nelson Miles. The Nez Perce War was over.

The Bannock War

There was a fourth incident in the same general area a year later when a series of conflicts erupted in 1878 between the Bannock and Northern Shoshone tribes and the United States. Again it was over a reservation treaty but one in which a whole region – the Camas prairie in Idaho – had been omitted from the treaty document in error. Camas is a plant with a blue or purple flower which has a nutritious bulb about the size and shape of a tulip bulb. Many tribes in the region used it as a major source of food and it was either eaten raw or steamed in a pit for immediate consumption. The camas bulbs could also be made into a dough which was shaped into loaves, wrapped in grass, and cooked. Without an adequate stock of camas, people would be ill prepared for the cold winter months.

Attempts to gather food from the Camas prairie was futile; the settlers had grazed their hogs there which had rooted out the bulbs. Deprived of their traditional food supplies and provided with inadequate supplies by the government the tribe was facing famine. Led by Chief Buffalo Horn some of the tribe left the reservation and joined with Northern Paiutes from the Malheur reservation under Chief Egan and began raiding

This image was used on one of Panarizon Publishing Corporation's 'Story of America' cards in 1979 and is stated to show some of Custer's soldiers posing with a Gatling at Fort Lincoln, Dakota Territory. Even allowing for distorted perspective, these appear to be 1in-calibre guns – very heavy and cumbersome, but ideal for use in or against fortified positions during a siege. If these are the ones Custer left behind when he went to the Little Bighorn it is not really surprising since they are not really suited to the mobile guerrilla warfare that seemed to characterize most US Army encounters with Native Americans. (Robert Forczyk)

settlements. Chief Buffalo Horn would have known that success was highly unlikely; he had served as a scout for Major General Howard during the Nez Perce War the previous year and the government set about aggressively quelling the uprising. Chief Buffalo Horn achieved victory in two battles but following what became the final battle in Idaho, the remaining tribe members surrendered.

One incident in this short campaign was noted by 1st Lieutenant John H. Parker, who later commanded the Gatlings at Santiago in 1898:

This campaign afforded one instance of the effective use of the .45 caliber Gatling gun against savages. A band of Bannocks and Shoshones were making a break for the Umatilla Agency, with a view to inducing the Indians at that place to go on the warpath. The 1st United States Cavalry, under Captain (subsequently Colonel) Bernard, went after them to prevent this. The regiment was accompanied by three of these Gatlings. They overhauled the hostiles near the Umatilla Agency, and the latter took refuge on a high bluff, which was commanded by ground equally high to the right. Three troops were dismounted as skirmishers and pushed forward to attack the bluff on which the Indians were lurking. On reaching the foot of the bluff, over an open space of about 600 yards, the skirmishers found themselves in front of a nearly vertical wall, at the top of which the Indians were lying and from which they began to pour in a most galling fire. The three troops were certain to suffer heavily if they retreated across the open ground, and were unable to climb the bluff in the face of the fire. Just as they were beginning to suffer heavily, the Gatlings opened from the high ground to the right, to which place they had been moved on a run, and the fire from the Indians on the bluff at once ceased. The fight was terminated by the defeat of the Indians, who were struck on their flank by another force as they left the bluff. There can be no doubt that these three troops would have suffered very heavily if they had not received the aid of the machine guns. This account of the skirmish is furnished by a participant. It will be observed that this is a typical use of the guns with cavalry, in either Indian or civilized warfare. To gain a flank and pour a sharp and unexpected fire upon the enemy is usually a decisive maneuver, and one particularly adapted to these guns. (Quoted in Wahl & Toppel 1966: 82)

Another feature common to the Indian campaigns was the presence of Nelson Miles, seen here on the cover of *Harper's Weekly*, 18 April 1891. He declared that Gatlings 'are worthless for Indian fighting' and asserted that 'The range is no longer than the rifle and the bullet so small that you cannot tell where they strike' (quoted in Cruse 2008: 48). A few years later Miles did employ the product of one of Gatling's rivals, the Hotchkiss revolving cannon, firing 37mm exploding shrapnel shells. In a master stroke of understatement Miles described their effects on the recipients of such fire as being 'very demoralising' (quoted in Hotchkiss 1880: 286)! (Anne S.K. Brown Military Collection, Brown University Library)

HARPER'S WEEKLY

JOURNAL OF CIVILIZATION

VOL. XXXV.—No. 1791.
Copyright, 1891, by Harper & Brothers. All rights reserved.

NEW YORK, SATURDAY, APRIL 18, 1891.

TEN CENTS A COPY. INCLUDING SUPPLEMENT.

GENERAL NELSON A. MILES.—From a Photograph by Taber, San Francisco.—[See Page 292.]

One feature of most of these campaigns was the nature of the engagements. Unlike the more or less static battles of the Civil War, the Indian Wars were more like guerrilla warfare, something the Army had not really encountered before. They were often running battles over many miles against incomparable horsemen who were able to hang onto and fire accurately under their horses' necks with very little of their bodies exposed. The Nez Perce War, for instance, was described by General William T. Sherman as 'one of the most extraordinary Indian Wars of which there is any record' (quoted in Wahl & Toppel 1966: 81). The Nez Perce bands under Chief Joseph numbered about 600, of whom only 200 or fewer were warriors. During the 11 weeks of the war, they travelled between 1,300 and 1,600 miles, and in 13 engagements defeated or fought to a stand-off ten separate US Army commands. This was not the sort of warfare, or terrain, where the Gatling could be put to much use. What little use the weapon did have was sporadic and, it would seem, sufficiently spectacular to be the subject of extensive official or popular commentary. It could not be claimed that they had played a decisive role.

The Spanish–American War

Just prior to 1898, Spanish colonial policy suspended constitutional guarantees to Cuban nationals and open revolt resulted. In the United States, sympathy for the rebels was widespread and when USS *Maine* was sunk by a mysterious explosion in Havana harbour on 15 February 1898, America was outraged and – convinced it was a Spanish act of aggression – demanded the Spanish leave the island. In response, Spain declared war on 24 April and in reply, America declared war the following day. The first engagement of this war actually occurred in the Philippines, which were under Spanish rule at that time, and though Gatlings were used, there seems very little contemporary commentary regarding them.

Men of the Gatling Detachment manhandling their guns and limber somewhere in Cuba. One of a pair of stereo-photographs published in 1898 by Strohmeyer & Wyman, New York. (Private collection)

An expeditionary force began to be assembled at Tampa, Florida, to oust the Spanish from Cuba. This coincided with the delivery to the US Army of 15 of the 100 new Gatling guns which had been ordered and which were adapted to fire the same .30in-calibre cartridge as the newly adopted Krag magazine rifle. 1st Lieutenant John H. Parker of the 13th Infantry proposed that to take advantage of this, a Gatling gun detachment be formed as part of this expeditionary force. In this he was strongly supported by an officer of the Ordnance Department in charge of the Ordnance Depot at Tampa, Lieutenant John T. Thompson, who was to design his own machine gun – the 'Tommy Gun' – a few years later. The result was the formation of the Gatling Detachment of the 5th Army Corps.

Many names became famous from this war, perhaps most prominent being the battle of San Juan Hill at Santiago and 'Teddy' Roosevelt and his 'Rough Riders', and there are a number of accounts of the effectiveness of the Gatlings and contemporary illustrations of them in action. During

San Juan Hill, 1 July 1898 (overleaf)

Although the US Army had the new Colt-Browning fully automatic 'machine gun' and used it in the Spanish–American War, it was the Gatlings which were credited with winning the day at San Juan Hill. The Gatlings were quickly brought up, unlimbered and while the gun and limber were being prepared and positioned for action, the two mules used to draw them would be taken to the rear, hopefully out of harm's way. Because the Spanish, equally well equipped and outnumbering the Americans two to one, were entrenched just at the crest of the hill, aiming directly at them would have been ineffective. A 'dropping' fire was needed so that the bullets came down into the trenches at a slight angle. To achieve that, and the range, combined with the fact they were firing uphill, the Gatlings would have had to be elevated quite significantly.

During the battle, the Gatlings fired approximately 18,000 rounds in 8½ minutes into the Spanish position. Each gun was manned by six to eight men, one firing the gun, another replenishing the magazine feed. The guns were fitted with the Bruce Feed system which meant the magazine could be continually replenished without having to interrupt the firing. Such a combined rate of fire from the guns would have needed men running back and forth to the limbers, each holding 9,600 cartridges, to collect supplies of the card boxes of ammunition specially made to feed the Bruce magazine easily and quickly. While the American forces had the advantage of much shorter supply lines than the Spanish because, by comparison, they were fighting on their own doorstep, they did have one important disadvantage. Their military system had ensured that all the firearms – rifles, Gatling guns and Colt-Browning machine guns – used a single type of cartridge, the .30-40 Krag, but they still had not adopted smokeless propellant for either small arms or artillery, whereas the Spanish had. All the firing from American guns, especially Gatlings and artillery, would produce clouds of smoke; even if shielded by shrubbery, it made them easy targets to spot for the Spanish gunners, and many of the Gatling crews would be killed or injured by shrapnel from exploding shells. In contrast, there were no giveaway signs of the Spanish gun positions, but the relentless fire from the Gatlings, steadily being pushed forward during the battle, killed or wounded many of the defenders of the hill and disrupted their fire on the American forces. Indeed, the Gatling fire falling on the Spanish position was so intense that the advancing US infantry had to hold back as they approached the crest of the hill until a cease-fire order could be given to the Gatlings; the infantry were then able to charge, overrun the Spanish positions and take the hill.

the battle, Parker's Gatling guns expended approximately 18,000 rounds in 8½ minutes (over 700 rounds per minute of continuous fire) into the Spanish defensive lines atop the heights, killing many of the defenders and forcing others to flee the trench lines, while disrupting the aim of any still alive who continued to resist (Armstrong 1982: 104). Colonel H.C. Egbert, commander of the 6th Infantry assaulting San Juan Hill, stated that his regiment was brought to a halt near the top of the hill to await the cease-fire order, as the Gatling fire striking the crest and trench line was so intense.

Theodore Roosevelt, in his preface to Parker's book, gave much of the credit for the capture of the Spanish on San Juan Hill to Parker and his Gatling detachment. During the attack on Kettle and San Juan hills, Roosevelt observed that the hammering sound of the guns raised the spirits of his men: 'While thus firing, there suddenly smote on our ears a peculiar drumming sound. One or two of the men cried out, "The Spanish machine guns!" but, after listening a moment, I leaped to my feet and called, "It's the Gatlings, men! Our Gatlings!" Immediately the troopers began to cheer lustily, for the sound was most inspiring.' And later, having taken the hills:

> ... the Spaniards became bolder, and made an attack on our position ... we at once ran forward to the crest and opened on them, and as we did so, the unmistakeable drumming of the Gatlings opened abreast of us, to our right, and the men cheered again ... I strolled over to find out about the Gatlings, and there I found Lieut. Parker with two of his guns right on our left, abreast of our men who at that time were closer to the Spanish than any others. From thence on, Parker's Gatlings were our inseparable companions throughout the siege. They were right up at the front. When we dug our trenches, he took off the wheels of his guns and put them in the trenches. At no hour, day or night, was Parker anywhere but where we wished him to be ... If a troop of my regiment was sent off to guard some road or a break in the lines, we were almost certain to get Parker to send a Gatling along ... at whatever hour of the twenty four the fighting began, the drumming of the Gatlings was soon heard through the cracking of our own carbines. (Parker 1898)

THE GATLING ABROAD

The widespread adoption of the Gatling outside the USA is made apparent by Captain Rogers' remark in his paper presented to the Royal United Services Institution in 1876: '... every state in Europe having adopted some type of machine gun ... even Turkey, Egypt, China, Japan, Tunis, Morocco have procured armaments of this description. Russia in particular possesses a formidable array – 400 Gatlings in 8 batteries attached to artillery' (Rogers 1875: 423). And, depending upon the accuracy of the accounts regarding Butler's Gatlings during the Bermuda Hundred campaign in the Civil War, it may be that the gun was first actually used in earnest on the battlefield in Europe.

The Franco-Prussian War

It is in the various accounts of the Franco-Prussian War that the widespread use of the ambiguous term *mitrailleuse* really makes itself apparent, resulting in uncertainty as to which weapon was actually being used. Gatling had not been slow to promote his gun among foreign powers and, for whatever reason, the French were possibly the first to be approached. As early as 29 October 1863 Gatling wrote to Major R. Maldon of the French Committee of Artillery in Paris describing his gun and asking for the information to be passed on to the Emperor. In the event, the French declined Gatling's offer and shortly after, the US Government banned the export of arms and munitions of war (Gatling 1870: 515).

By the time of the Franco-Prussian War it would appear that France had obtained a number of Gatlings, although Fletcher tells us the 'Gatling was very little used by the French' (Fletcher 1872: 40). This view is supported by Captain Rogers, who suggests 'A few Gatlings were, it is true, employed in the campaigns of Le Mans, and at the siege of Paris' but then goes on to say that 'they must have been of a crude and obsolete pattern, for the emperor some time previous to the war refused to purchase 100 Gatlings of an improved model offered him by the Gatling Gun Company' (Rogers 1875: 421fn). These may indeed have been the version of the Model 1862 gun in which the loading chambers had been modified to accept metallic cartridges. One account leaves no ambiguity regarding the weapon but, frustratingly, does not specify the particular engagement in which it was used:

Up to this time we had not seen any Prussians beyond a few skirmishers in the plain, though our battery of Gatlings had kept blazing away at nothing in particular all the while; but now an opportunity of its being in use occurred. A column of troops appeared in the valley below us, coming from the right – a mere dark streak upon the white snow; but no one in the battery could tell whether they were friends or foes, and the commander hesitated about opening fire. But now an aide-de-camp came dashing down the hill with orders to pound them at once – a French journalist, it seems, having discovered them to be enemies, when the general and all his staff were as puzzled as ourselves. Rr-rr-a go our Gatlings, the deadly hail of bullets crushes into the thick of them, and slowly back into the woods the dark mass retires, leaving, however, a trace of black dots upon the white snow behind it. This, their famous and 4 o'clock effort and its failure, has decided the day. That one discharge was enough. (Quoted in Hamilton 1888: 886)

A detail from an illustration showing French troops with a *mitrailleuse* battery being readied for dispatch from Paris via the Strasbourg railway. *Illustrated London News*, 6 August 1870, p. 140. (Private collection)

One American magazine (see page 1) shows a group of Prussian soldiers examining a captured Gatling, which at least provides supporting evidence for their use by the French, but again there is no reference to the engagement in which they were captured. For some reason, the Prussians had not been favourably impressed by the Gatling but it was suggested that 'their late experiences have probably changed their opinion' (Brockett 1871: 98). On the other hand, the Prussians were content with their superiority in numbers, discipline, and their 'secret' weapon, the *Zündnadelgewehr* (needlefire rifle) invented by Nikolaus von Dreyse, and dispensed with multifiring guns, except in the Bavarian contingent, by whom 'a nondescript species of revolving cannon was nevertheless at times used very effectively' (Rogers 1875: 421).

This was the Feldl, a four-barrelled 11mm-calibre gun capable of 300 rounds per minute, used quite effectively by German officer Hermann Graf Thürheim in defence of the village of Culmiers on 11 October 1870. He opened fire on French infantry at a range of 700–800yd, forcing them to retreat. He then turned the weapons on an enemy artillery battery at 1,200yd, prompting the French gunners to retreat beyond the range of the Feldl guns. However, during these actions, several barrels of Thürheim's guns had become unserviceable, due to faults with the ammunition feed system used, and he was forced to retire – partly because of these mechanical problems, but also due to a general German retreat in the face of superior French numbers. Nevertheless, in spite of the mechanical problems, Thürheim states that his original opinion on the value of the Feldl had been strengthened by his experience of them in war. Having said that, Thürheim goes on to express the view that

'Von der Tann's Mitrailleur', from Brockett 1871, facing p. 296. (Private collection)

The fire of the infantry ... will usually be much more effective than that of the battery, owing chiefly to the greater ease with which the individual rifleman can take advantage of the nature of the ground to get under cover. The Revolver-cannon will, therefore, be of little use in war, except in those cases in which, from insufficiency of cover, infantry cannot be deployed. (Quoted in Baring 1874: 28–30)

It also appears that General der Infanterie von der Tann, who commanded I. Bayerisches Armeekorps, had his own secret weapon in the form of a volley gun which seemed to owe more to earlier technology than any of the more recent weapons. It certainly had more than a passing resemblance to the 'organ guns' of old. So, despite knowing that Gatlings were used – by the French at least – in the Franco-Prussian War, there is little commentary, detailed or otherwise, on where they were employed, or their effectiveness.

The Gatling in Russian service

In Russia it was the practice to attach the name of the officer responsible for the adoption or acceptance of weapons into service to that weapon. In the case of the Gatling, that fell to General Alexander Gorloff, the military attaché at the Russian Embassy in Washington, DC (Rogers 1875: 421). Some later changes, suggested by an engineer named Baron008i, were overseen by the Nobel brothers and likewise their names became associated with the Gatling. Having these names inscribed on the guns has led to some confusion and the belief that they were new and different weapons, or spurious claims to the invention, which they were not.

We have seen from earlier comments that by 1876 Russia had 'a formidable array ... 400 Gatlings in 8 batteries attached to artillery' and some of these were put to use. After one of Russia's failed attempts at expansion had resulted in the Crimean War (1853–56), efforts towards empire-building and colonization were resurrected again and from 1864 to 1876 Russia pushed her boundaries beyond her neighbour's borders with military advances into Central Asia, resulting eventually in 1881 in the annexation of the whole Transcaspian region. One episode in this colonial expansion was the assault on the city of Khiva, in what is now Uzbekistan, which fell on 28 May 1873. Two Gatlings were employed and a Captain Litvinoff, who was responsible for them, reports:

about 3pm parties of horsemen began to appear and behind them larger masses – commenced to engage our pickets – one of these pickets, composed of 1 officer and 5 Cossacks, sword in hand, threw themselves forward against an approaching mass of Turkomans and were completely cut to pieces. Two companies of the 3rd battalion of sharpshooters and two battery guns [Gatlings] were ordered forward – the road we had to follow was very difficult even for infantry and cavalry as at every step we had to cross wide ditches, dug for irrigation, which had abrupt sides; for artillery the road would have been impossible. Our light battery guns went on this road with perfect ease, the ammunition packhorses alone giving us some trouble. When we

A Russian .42in Berdan Gatling gun and rifle cartridge, made by the Union Metallic Cartridge Company. (US National Park Service, Springfield Armory National Historic Site Photograph)

47

stopped a line of sharpshooters and battery guns was formed along one of these ditches – at a range of 1,050 to 1,170 yards. Opening at the first I fired rapidly 25 rounds; the band immediately dispersed, part of the men joining the second band. Opening from the second gun, I fired 50 rounds without interruption; the second band dispersed at once, and the men betook themselves to broken ground ... Several times the enemy collecting in masses of some strength moved against us, but each time was driven back by our fire; thus I had several opportunities of firing a succession of 25 or 50 rounds ... In the whole the battery guns fired that day 408 cartridges. (Quoted in Rogers 1875: 424)

On another occasion in this campaign, the Russians were assailed at 3am by Turcomans. According to the Russian officer in charge of the detachment:

At the first howls of the enemy ... leaving with the battery guns the most indispensable men to assist in firing ... I took myself the crank-handle of the first gun and invited Captain Cachourin to take the handle of the other gun, and enjoined on all my group not to commence fire before the word of command was given ... We had not long to wait. The cries of the Turcomans ... suddenly rose from all sides and became deafening. Though it was dark we perceived in front of us the galloping masses of the enemy with uplifted glittering swords. When they approached us within about twenty paces, I shouted the command

Based on the 1872 patent, this gun was used in the US Ordnance Department trials of 1873–74 to test Gatling guns of large calibre (1in) against rifle-calibre guns and howitzers firing shrapnel and similar multiple projectiles. It was concluded that the Gatling would have utility in situations where accurately placed, high-volume fire was required. From *OM* §17 Fig. 1, facing p. 60. (Private collection)

'Fire!' This was followed by a salvo of all the men forming the cover, and a continuous simultaneous rattle of the two battery guns. In this roar the cries of the enemy at once became weak, and then ceased altogether, vanishing as rapidly as they arose. The firing at once stopped, and as no enemy was visible, I ventured to get a look at the surrounding ground, availing myself of the first light of dawn. At some distance to the right of our square stood the 8th Battalion of the line. Between it and us, at every step, lay prostrated the dead bodies of the Yonoods. (Quoted in Rogers 1875: 438)

Yonoods may be a Russian term for Turcoman cavalry but no translation or definition has been found.

THE GATLING IN BRITISH SERVICE

It is possible that the most extensive use of the Gatling outside the USA was by Great Britain. In 1867, a Gatling was obtained and tried against a 9-pdr rifled breech-loading field gun firing shrapnel with encouraging results (War Office 1877: 376), followed in 1869 by a comparative trial with the Montigny *mitrailleuse*. Further experiments in 1870 resulted in preference being given to the Gatling, a decision later reinforced by the reports of officers present with the French or German armies during the Franco-Prussian War regarding the performance of the *mitrailleuse*. In 1871 it was recommended that guns of .65in calibre be adopted for naval and coastal-defence use and the smaller .45in-calibre gun for field service, plus some smaller .45in guns for Indian service. Some of the naval Gatlings in both calibres had already been made by W. Armstrong at the Elswick Ordnance Company; before more were made it was decided to test them in service and even though they were not finally approved for service until July or August 1874 (*LoC* §2647), they had their trial in the Third Anglo-Ashanti War of 1873–74.

In 1867 one of the Model 1865 guns in 1in calibre was brought to England by Major General John Love and Lewis Broadwell, agents for its sale in Europe, for demonstration to and inspection by the Select Committee on Ordnance, and for testing against an Armstrong gun firing caseshot, at the official ranges at Shoeburyness. Further experiments with improved guns led to official approval being given to the limited adoption of the improved Gatling in 1870, and which were ultimately manufactured to British Government requirements by W.G. Armstrong & Co. of Newcastle. As reported in the *Illustrated London News* of 23 March 1867: 'The Gatling gun is a formidable weapon; and for trenches, or a breach and for street fighting, would do execution. The little amount of recoil and the consequent advantage of retaining a tolerably accurate direction after being once sighted, might prove a valuable element, and, in certain cases, would give it an advantage not possessed by ordinary cannon, which have to be resighted after each discharge.' *Illustrated London News*, 23 March 1867, p. 300. (Private collection)

The Third Anglo-Ashanti War

Although the Gatling first saw active service in the Third Anglo-Ashanti War, its actual use seems to have been along similar lines to those of Ben Butler's in the American Civil War, limited to a demonstration of its destructive power to the Ashanti king and his counsellors. Following years of Ashanti raids, British colonial expansion on the Gold Coast precipitated a major Ashanti invasion which overwhelmed the Gold Coast tribes and the small British garrison was helpless. Sir Garnet Wolseley was appointed governor of the Gold Coast and given substantial reinforcements. *The Times* of 6 October 1873 observed:

> The Gatling guns which accompany the expedition are those known as the 0.45 inch. They will be mounted on carriages somewhat similar to the guns [i.e. artillery], and, we presume, are mainly intended for the defence of stockade positions. If by any lucky chance Sir Garnet Wolseley manages to catch a good mob of savages in the open, and at a moderate distance, he cannot do better than treat them to a little Gatling music. When well served the machine gun is terribly effective at distances from 400 to 600 yards ... a perfect rain of bullets may issue from the ten muzzles ... Altogether, we cannot wish the Ashantees worse luck than to get in the way of a Gatling well served ...

It is possible that these Gatlings, like many of those used later, were actually manned by men of the Naval Brigade which, as described in Rudyard Kipling's poem, 'Soldier an' Sailor Too', were sailors specially trained and deployed for land-based warfare. However, in the event, Gatlings did not need to be used in earnest. Sir Garnet Wolseley had received a group of Ashanti peace envoys from Kofi Karikari (King Kofi)

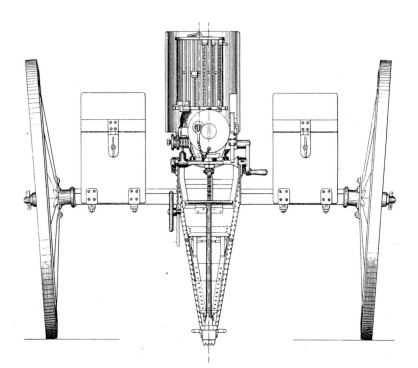

A rear view of the British service field carriage, made at the Royal Carriage Department, part of the Royal Gun Factory at Woolwich Arsenal. Note the inclusion of a shield for the drum magazine, a feature which does not seem to have appeared on the ones used in service. From Fletcher 1872, plate II. (Private collection)

British Gatling ammunition

In British service, .65in and .45in guns were used, but in contrast with most other countries, the unsystematic variety of ammunition used with the .45in gun still creates confusion. The specification for .65in cartridge with coiled brass cases, approved in 1875 (*LoC* §3324), never changed and by 1881 the .65in Gatling had been practically superseded by the 1in Nordenfelt, though no accounts mentioning this Gatling being used by the Royal Navy have been encountered (War Office 1881: 340).

While developing .45in Gatling cartridges for British service, logic seems to have been abandoned. Even when the 'Boxer' cartridge for the Snider rifle was created, the technology for manufacturing stronger, more durable and re-usable solid-drawn cases was available from the United States. Even so, the British military authorities stuck with their flimsy 'coiled' cases of brass foil. Gatling himself observed that making the Boxer case was more complicated than making a solid-drawn case from a single piece of brass or copper, and the metallic case could be manufactured as cheaply. The Superintendent of the Royal Laboratory, where British ammunition was produced, however, baulked at costs of new tooling (*DAS* §2873). The Special Committee on Mitrailleurs very sensibly noted that as the introduction of a new rifle of .45in calibre was imminent, ammunition for the Gatling and the new rifle should be interchangeable. But ten years after the introduction of the Martini-Henry rifle, that eminently sensible point was still being contested (see Committee on Machine Guns 1880).

An alternative sample cartridge was submitted by a Captain Noble but the only details discovered are that it was of Boxer construction with a case made of tin plate, 33 Standard Wire Gauge (.008in) thick, and of .5/.45in form. However, the Committee abandoned the use of the Boxer .45in cartridge in the Gatling, settling on a solid-drawn case with the same .45in bullet and charge as the Martini-Henry cartridge, as noted in *LoC* §2644, July and December 1873, and modified in March 1874 by adding another cannelure to the bullet. This was the 'Cartridge, Small Arm, Ball, Gatling, 0.45 inch bore, Mark I' and with solid-drawn case and two fire holes in the cap chamber, it followed the Berdan form of cartridge construction.

In 1878 a special cartridge was produced for use with Gatling guns in India – 'Cartridge, Small Arm, Ball, Gatling, 0.45 inch, light, Mark I' (*LoC* §3470) – having bullet and powder weights reduced to 410 grains and 80 grains respectively and the case shortened by .155in. This is the cartridge shown in the illustration at bottom right and designated as 'mountain gun'. A Mark II version of the standard cartridge was introduced in 1882 and designated as

LEFT An example of the experimental .4in cartridge which was abandoned in the light of a new .303in-calibre bolt-action magazine rifle being developed using smokeless propellant. (Private collection)

ABOVE The standard Boxer .577/.45 Martini-Henry cartridge. Its flimsy construction was always a source of problems, especially when a soldier was trying to load cartridges that had become distorted in his cartridge pouches. (Private collection)

'Cartridge, Machine Gun, Ball, Gardner and Gatling, .45 inch' (*LoC* §4193). However, it was discovered that Gatling guns had to be adjusted to handle this slightly altered cartridge. In 1886 the situation was complicated further by designating the Mark II cartridge as 'Cartridge, Machine Gun, Ball, Gardner, Gatling and Nordenfelt .45 inch, except Martini-Henry chambered guns' (*LoC* §5023). The List of Changes entry goes on to note that the cartridge will be used with .45in machine guns 'except those having Martini-Henry chamber, which take the Mark II solid case for Martini-Henry rifle' (*LoC* §5023). So, eventually, some machine guns *were* chambered for the Martini-Henry cartridge!

The confusion surrounding ammunition was officially acknowledged in 1888 with instructions issued (*LoC* §5577) that brass labels designating the appropriate cartridge were to be attached to the various guns. Further confusion arose in the early 1880s when .4in-calibre rifles were contemplated. This all came to naught since many European powers were adopting magazine-fed bolt-action rifles, and the quantum leap of 1884 with the French development of smokeless powders and an even smaller-bore, high-velocity rifle in 1886 dictated the future. Nevertheless, the British for some perverse reason decided to adapt machine guns to the .4in cartridge, but it was never formally approved and remained an experimental diversion. (A series of articles on British Gatling cartridges can be found in *Guns Review*, September 1980: 675; November 1980: 867; July 1982: 605; November 1986: 759–60; and December 1986: 830 & 832.)

BELOW In 1884, Kynoch's, the ammunition manufacturers of Birmingham, England, were advertising a variety of Gatling cartridges in their catalogue. The manufacture of such things as the 1in and .75in as shown in this catalogue would suggest there was a demand for them somewhere outside of Britain. From left to right: 1in ball, long; .75in; .65in; .45in Field Gun; .45in Mountain Gun. (Private collection)

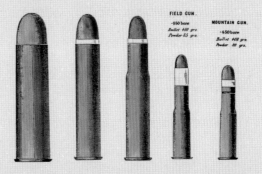

and, according to one account, published in the *London Daily News* on 27 January 1874: 'On the fourth day they were allowed to see the practice with the Gatling guns. That night one of the Ashantee escorts shot himself. It afterwards appeared that he had been so frightened by the Gatling shot that he had said if white men had those weapons, resistance was useless.'

As reported in the *Army & Navy Journal* of 7 March 1874: 'We are not surprised that the Ashantees were awe-struck before the power of the Gatling gun. It is easy to understand that it is a weapon which is specially adapted to terrify a barbarous or semi-civilized foe.' The same article quotes the Ashanti correspondent of the *New York Herald* who tells that the reputation of the Gatling is now spread throughout Ashanti and in the words of one Ashanti dignitary: 'it is a terrible gun which shoots all day. Nothing can stand before it: the water of the Prah ran back affrighted.' He goes on to say, 'The effects of this, combined with many other things, has been to induce the King and his Council to deliberate and reflect on the possibility of peace' (Featherstone 1978: 58). Despite this, the Ashanti king continued his raids, so, with British regiments and native levies, in February 1874 Wolseley entered Kumasi, the Ashanti capital, and razed it. Britain then withdrew from Ashanti lands.

The South Pacific

Chronologically, the Gatling's next use was by the Royal Navy in May 1877, in a skirmish with the Peruvian ironclad, *Huáscar*. She had been built for the Peruvian Government by Laird Brothers at Birkenhead for use in the war against Spain and was launched on 7 October 1865 but, after fitting out, arrived too late to participate. However, during the Peruvian Civil War of 1877, rebels, led by retired Captain Germán Astete and with the aid of two Carrasco brothers who were lieutenants in the Peruvian Navy, commandeered the ship. She was used to harass, sabotage and disrupt government forces and also allegedly used in acts of piracy against British merchant ships. The Peruvian Navy failed to capture or destroy her in a 90-minute engagement and the British *chargé-d'affaires* at Lima sent for the British Pacific squadron under the command of Rear Admiral de Horsey. He pursued *Huáscar* in his flagship, HMS *Shah*, an unarmoured wooden corvette, along with HMS *Amethyst*. Overtaking her on 29 May 1877 just off the port of Ylo, he demanded her surrender. This was refused by the rebel leader Nicolás de Piérola, who was on board, and what is sometimes referred to as the battle of Pacocha commenced. After exchanging fire with conventional guns, the British vessels closed on their opponent. According to the *Illustrated London News* of 21 July 1877:

> About five o'clock the *Huáscar* being clear of the shoals, we seized the opportunity to close. The enemy also closed with evident signs of ramming, firing shell from her 40-pounder. Our Gatling gun then commenced firing from the foretop, causing the men on her upper-deck quarters to desert their guns. Our port guns immediately commenced 'independent firing'. A Whitehead torpedo was fired at the moment of passing, but as the *Huáscar* at that instant altered course ... the torpedo failed to reach her.

Apart from possibly being the first recorded use of a foretop-mounted Gatling, and probably the only ship-to-ship engagement of the Royal Navy between 1850 and 1914, this engagement is also of interest in being the first in which the Whitehead self-propelled torpedo was used, the first in which a British warship engaged an ironclad and the first instance of wooden ships engaging a turret ship. Although *Huáscar* escaped, she was captured two days later by the Peruvian Navy and was repaired, and the Peruvians having learnt from experience, she was equipped with Gatling guns. Two years later, in October 1879, during the South Pacific War she was captured and entered the service of the Chilean Navy. In 1995, the World Ship Trust gave the Maritime Heritage Award to the Chilean Navy for its restoration of *Huáscar*, berthed after many years of service at the port of Talcahuano, Chile. *Huáscar*, along with HMS *Warrior*, is one of the few early ironclad-era warships to survive, and one of the few still afloat.

A foretop-mounted Gatling in action on a British ship, although the artist has incorrectly shown the gun firing from a barrel at the 12 o'clock position instead of the 8 o'clock position. It is also questionable whether the gravity feed from the drum would work at such a steep depression, or that the drum would not fall off, without assistance. *Illustrated London News*, 2 March 1878, p. 189. (Private collection)

The Second Anglo-Afghan War

In November 1878 a threatened war between Britain and Russia became a real war with Afghanistan when the British invaded to suppress the ruling dynasty, which was becoming too friendly with Russia for British liking. The first phase of the war ended in May 1879 with the Treaty of Gandamak, which created a new Afghan leadership but gave Britain control over Afghanistan's foreign policy. It was an uneasy peace and in September 1879 an anti-British uprising in Kabul led to further hostilities which ended a year later in September 1880 with the decisive battle of Kandahar. Gatlings were used in this war, though their performance was neither decisive nor inspiring. However, that may have been the result of inexperience and youthful enthusiasm. The young Lieutenant John Adye of the Royal Artillery, soon after arriving in Rawalpindi where he was to instruct gunners in the use of a new mountain artillery 'screw gun' – a term applied to a mountain gun in which the barrel was in two sections for ease of transport by pack animal, and screwed together for use, first issued for use in Afghanistan in 1879 (War Office 1893: 75). Adye received a telegram from Colonel Murray, Assistant Adjutant General for Royal Artillery in India and a friend of his father's, asking if he knew anything about Gatling guns. In his own words:

A photograph of the two Gatlings and their crews during the Second Anglo-Afghan War. Lieutenant Adye may be the officer in the centre of the photograph. Note the very narrow carriages, the unusual shape of the barrel plates and the presence of a central one. (Courtesy of the Council of the National Army Museum, London, neg 6315TN)

Now my knowledge of them was confined to the facts that a Gatling consisted of a number of rifle barrels stuck together, surmounted by a sort of drum, or cartridge carrier, which, with the barrels, was actuated by a handle, which, turning, made the barrels revolve, supplied them with cartridges from the drum, and fired each barrel in turn ... of the detailed mechanism of the machine I knew nothing, but I did not hesitate to reply that I was well acquainted with the Gatling gun, for I guessed what was the object of the enquiry. Sure enough, in a few days' time came an order from Army Headquarters for me to proceed at once to Kuram, in Afghanistan – the Headquarters of the Kuram

Valley Field Force, then commanded by a rising soldier, Major-General Frederick Roberts, R.A., there to take command of a couple of Gatling guns ... here was a command all to myself, an unexpected piece of good luck for a young subaltern of one and twenty. (Adye 1925: 28–30)

Adye had hardly arrived in Kuram before Roberts asked for a demonstration. Adye reports: 'The result was a complete fiasco. The handles worked so stiffly and caused so much "jump" at each revolution, as to throw the gun off the target with the result that the bullets went everywhere except where they should have gone.' He felt, with some justification, that he could hardly be blamed for the failure, having only seen the guns two days before with no time to overhaul them or get his men trained in the handling of them. So it was probably not the fault of the guns or the men but of the haste! However, his claim that 'the two Gatlings ... were of an antiquated pattern' can hardly be justified since they had only been adopted into service some four years previously and the photograph on page 54 shows the guns, if not the carriages, to be those in service at that time. From the illustration it is evident that the guns had a very narrow wheel-base which must have made them very unstable. However, there is a photograph showing the Gatlings dismantled and mounted on pack animals, which suggests the wheeled carriages were perhaps less for transportation and more for ease of manoeuvring and manipulating when in use.

Although Roberts took the failure in his stride, he did not trust the Gatlings to stop a charge of fanatical Afghans. Adye's further association with them also seems obscure. Since he tells us he 'believed' the only time they were used was near the Shutugurdan Pass where they failed ignominiously and were deposited in an arsenal at Kabul, it has to be assumed he was not with them. Another account published in the *Illustrated London News* of 21 February 1880, however, shows that they were used in the defence of the Sherpore Cantonment, a fortified British camp in Kabul, but there is no commentary on their performance.

The fortified Sherpore Cantonment. Note the Gatling on the right. Though this is not an accurate image, the narrow carriage is again evident and not a piece of artistic misrepresentation. *Illustrated London News*, 21 February 1880, p. 185. (Private collection)

The Anglo-Zulu War

About the same time that Gatlings were being decried in Afghanistan, they were giving much better accounts of themselves in Africa. In 1852 Britain had renounced its sovereignty over the Transvaal region which then became the South African Republic. 25 years later, Britain changed its mind and annexed it again. This was explained as a step towards 'bringing unity to South Africa'. There was no mention of the fact that in the meantime, diamonds and gold had both been discovered in the Transvaal. In this step, Britain also inherited the border disputes between the Zulu and the Boers and, having issued the Zulu king, Cetshwayo, an ultimatum in December 1878, which he declined, war began in January 1879. As the Commander-in-Chief of the British Army, HRH the Duke of Cambridge observed: 'Nowhere, either in Southern or Central Africa, did such a powerfully organised, well-disciplined and thoroughly trained force of courageous men exist as lay at the disposal of Ketchwayo [*sic*]' (quoted in Lock & Quantrill 2005: 20).

There are numerous references to the Gatlings in accounts of the various engagements in this war but few give any detail of their use and effectiveness and, despite the superiority of British technology in arms, it quickly became apparent that it was not going to be an easy victory for Britain. No sooner

Men of the Naval Brigade from HMS *Tenedos* practising with their Gatling at Fort Pearson. *Illustrated London News*, 8 March 1879, p. 213. (Private collection)

had war started than the massacre at Isandlwana occurred, a defeat the like of which the British Army had never suffered before. On the same day, a column commanded by Colonel Charles Pearson and moving in from Fort Pearson on the Tugela River near the coast toward Eshowe, was ambushed at the Nyezane River. In the words of an unidentified young officer quoted in the *Penny Illustrated Paper* of 22 March 1879:

> ... at 7.30 we had just halted for breakfast when we hear all at once firing straight in front, and found that the native levies who formed the advanced guard had been attacked by Zulus. There was a little hill quite free from bush on our left. G and F companies immediately took possession of it and lay down about ten yards from the crest. The bush lay stretched out in front of us on a low plain, out of which the Zulus were keeping up a good fire. The two guns and two rocket tubes of the Naval Brigade were just behind us on the crest, firing over our heads. The Zulus fought splendidly, for they kept up the fire out of the bush for two hours while we poured vollies [*sic*] into them from the hill at 300 yards.

This commentary may be being misinterpreted; a later account of the defence of Eshowe refers to only one Gatling being in the camp (Lloyd 1881: 454), and the same young officer quoted above, in referring to the Naval Brigade, which was from HMS *Active*, enthuses: 'Jack [i.e. Jack Tar, a sailor] distinguished himself on this occasion by bringing the Gatling into action the first time on land.' Gatling is referred to in the singular, and the claim for the first use on land does not stand up to scrutiny, but his further comments no one could dispute: 'The student of military history will remember with what destructive effect the French used their Mitrailleur, and mowed down whole ranks of Teutons during the Franco-German war. Our Gatlings are not less serviceable, as was ably proved by Midshipman Coker on the occasion under notice.' In his own report of the event, quoted in the same newspaper, Midshipman Lewis Coker states:

> Sir, – I have the honour to report I was placed in rear of the leading column with Gatling gun. About two hours and a half after leaving the camping-grounds the head of the column was engaged. A report having come in that the natives were threatening the rear of the column, I placed my gun on a hill, in a good position for firing if necessary. I brought my gun into action ... no natives appearing I moved on with the wagons ... on arriving at the foot of the hill, where the headquarters were, I was ordered by Colonel Pearson to bring the gun up and place it opposite a hill where some natives had taken up a position. I immediately opened fire on them; they retiring in the bush, I ceased firing, having expended about 300 rounds.

The *Army and Navy Gazette* of 22 February 1879 noted:

> The Gatling guns, landed with the naval contingent from the *Active* and *Tenedos*, have astonished the Zulus who have been trying an

engagement with our blue jackets. They found the fire much too hot, and the naval force have had the satisfaction of carrying more than one contested position. It is a pity that Gatlings are not more plentiful with Lord Chelmsford's army. The naval brigade have got some but the artillery have none. If there had been a couple of Gatlings with the force annihilated the other day, the result of the fight might have been different, for Gatlings are the best of all engines of war to deal with the rush of a dense crowd.

Note this refers to Gatling 'guns' in the plural. Soon after Pearson's force had arrived in Eshowe 'young Coker of the "Active", the midshipman who was so popular amongst us all, died of dysentery. He was a fine young fellow, beloved by his men, and only eighteen years old. His burial was the most affecting sight I ever witnessed in my short life; there were very few dry eyes' (Lloyd 1881: 461). The siege of Eshowe lasted just over eight weeks and was relieved by a force led by Lord Chelmsford which set out on 29 March, crossing the Tugela River in the early morning. The following day they laagered on the banks of the 40yd-wide Amatikulu River and spent nearly all of 31 March crossing it; 1 April saw the column change direction and head towards Eshowe. After 5 miles, the wagons were laagered at Ginginlovu. Reveille was sounded at 4am on 2 April, possibly as a result of scouts having observed Zulu crossing the Nyezane River. The traditional square was formed to await the attack. It was roughly 130yd on each side, manned by 3,000 white troops and about 2,500 Native troops. Lord Chelmsford's relief party was reinforced by naval brigades from HMS *Shah* and HMS *Boadicea* equipped with artillery, rockets and Gatlings. The naval brigades' artillery was placed at each corner with a rocket battery on the north-east corner facing the Nyezane River. Gatlings were placed at the south-east and south-west corners. It is estimated that around 8,000 Zulu mounted the attack. As they moved in on the four flanks of the square, Commander J. Brackenbury in charge of the Gatlings asked to be allowed to test the range. Captain W.C.F. Molyneux, a staff officer, reported: 'The Chief [Chelmsford], who was close by, did not object to the range being tested, providing he stopped at once. A final sight and, I am sure, quite two turns of the handle was the response, and there was a clear lane cut right through the body of men ...' (Molyneux 1896: 132). In the words of Captain T.E. Hutton of the 3/60th Rifles:

> The Zulus continued to advance, still at a run, when they began to open fire. In spite of the excitement of the moment we could not but admire the perfect manner in which these Zulus skirmished. A small knot of five or six would rise and dart through the long grass, dodging from side to side with heads down, rifles and shields kept low and out of our sight. They would then suddenly sink into the long grass and

The fortified encampment at Ginginlovu with the men of HMS *Shah* manning the Gatling gun and the ramparts. Obviously the artist had not quite come to grips with the construction and appearance of the Gatling, and interestingly, the men are shown armed with muzzle-loading short Enfield rifles, not Martini-Henrys. *Illustrated London News*, 24 May 1879, p. 477. (Private collection)

nothing but puffs of curling smoke would show their whereabouts. Then they advanced again and their bullets soon began to whistle merrily over our heads or strike the little parapet in front. We had been ordered to reserve our fire, and then fire by volleys at 400 yards distance. The Gatling had begun, however, and it was with difficulty that I could make the order to fire be heard by my company. (Quoted in Lock & Quantrill 2005: 147)

By 7.15am, after an hour of fierce fighting, the Zulu attack wavered. They began to withdraw and the bugle sounded 'cease firing'. Lord Chelmsford reported:

... two Gatling guns accompanied the column, and at the battle of Ginginlovu did considerable execution amongst the Zulus at the opening of their attack, which commenced on the north side of our position. The Zulus very soon, however, worked round to the west and south sides of our laager and the Gatlings were not in action therefore for any great length of time. (Quoted in Beresford 1884: 947)

It is estimated that 1,200 Zulu were killed; British losses were six regulars and seven of the Natal Native Contingent killed. With the Zulu defeat at Ginginlovu, combined with that at Kambula a few days previously, King Cetshwayo was ready to negotiate peace but Chelmsford was having none of that. There was the score of Isandlwana to settle and that he would not negotiate. In the mean time, reinforcements, sent out from Britain after the

A fine study of the two Gatlings of the Royal Artillery, fitted with fully loaded Broadwell drum magazines, which took part in the battle of Ulundi. Army guns were mounted on a heavier carriage than their Royal Navy counterparts – note the boxes on the axle trees for carrying spare ammunition which the RN carriages lacked. (Courtesy of the Council of the National Army Museum, London, neg 84858TN)

news of Isandlwana, had eventually arrived, including four Royal Artillery Gatling guns under the command of Major Owen, and Chelmsford readied himself for another, and final, offensive.

After various probing forays, Chelmsford gathered his commanders at Fort Nolela on the Umfolozi River on 3 July and told them that the river was to be crossed in force the following day. At 3.45am, the troops 'stood to' in silence and at 5.45am, a column led by Buller crossed the river and fanned out to shield the remaining columns from attack as they advanced toward the Ulundi Plain where they were to form a square. At 7.30am, orders were given to begin forming the square, which was 300–400yd long and 150yd wide and comprised just over 5,000 men (Brown 1881: 153).

Masses of Zulu were soon seen all around at a distance of 2,000–3,000yd. One of the four attacking Zulu forces was estimated at 8,000 men. They quickly advanced on all sides of the square and their firing became quite heavy but was not well aimed, most passing over the heads of the men in the square. The Gatling crews came into action and lost two men wounded but fired about 3,000 rounds, even though they jammed several times. Brown also comments 'the effect of the Gatlings was not so great as its admirers expected, but against skirmishers in the open was not a favourable opportunity for it' (Brown 1881: 156). Another commentary suggests that the jamming was initially thought to be caused by bolts dropping out, which seems a very unlikely occurrence, unless the lock-removal plug which passes through the cascable had been removed or lost; a more likely cause was trying to fire the guns too quickly for the

Brevet Lieutenant-Colonel Owen – who commanded the Gatlings at Ulundi – demonstrating how they were fired. British troops were formed in a square during the battle, with the Gatlings on the front face; their fire proved devastating against the Zulu attack on that side. Even so, their performance was erratic, for the bolts of both guns slipped out several times during the action, and firing had to cease while their crews searched for them in the long grass. Note how the guns hitched to the limber. The boxes on the axletrees used for carrying Broadwell drum magazines are clearly visible, the one on the left with its lid open being the one for the drum on the gun; the limber was used for additional magazines plus tools and spares necessary for the maintenance of the guns. (Courtesy of the Council of the National Army Museum, London, neg 23824TN)

gravity feed from the magazines to function properly (Lock & Quantrill 2005: 262). Lord Chelmsford observed:

> At Ulundi also we had two Gatlings in the centre of the front face of our square. They jammed several times in the action but when in work proved a very valuable addition to the strength of our defences on that flank. The Gatlings however required too much care in firing and could not be entrusted to any but skilled manipulators; if a machine gun can be invented that may safely be entrusted to infantry soldiers to work, and could be fired very much as one grinds an organ, I am satisfied of its great value. (Quoted in Beresford 1884: 947)

Ulundi was the decisive battle in the Anglo-Zulu War. King Cetshwayo fled, but his capture a few weeks later brought the war to an end.

Egypt and the Sudan

Although Egypt's influence on Europe extends over more than 5,000 years, its strategic importance to European powers began to develop in the 18th century as Britain gained more and more influence over India from the French. To get to India it was possible to travel wholly by sea but it was quicker to follow the old trade routes, using the port of Alexandria and the Red Sea or the Gulf of Suez as the interchange. Although a short overland journey was needed, it was still substantially quicker than sailing all the way round the Cape. The Suez Canal, which opened in 1869, was enormously successful and swiftly became vital to Britain's commercial interests.

In 1875 it became apparent that the Khedive, Ismail Pasha, in his attempts to 'modernize' Egypt along European lines, had incurred a huge debt of around £100 million. The only way the creditors could be kept at bay was by raising money and the British Government grasped the initiative by buying Egypt's shares in the Suez Canal Company. Almost overnight, the British effectively gained control of the canal and her political influence grew considerably. As British and French influence became more marked, Egypt's growing loss of sovereignty was so keenly felt by many Egyptians that in 1882 Colonel Ahmed Arabi Pasha initiated a revolt from inside the Egyptian Army. On Sunday, 11 June, Egyptians rioted in Alexandria and killed about 50 Europeans including three British military personnel. Despite France's wish to stay neutral, Britain took the initiative and responded by bombarding Alexandria on 11 July. The physical effect of the bombardment on the port's defences were slight. It was followed, however, by a far greater destructive effect on morale when the Naval Brigade landed, as recounted by Captain Lord Charles Beresford RN:

> When the Gatling guns were landed at Alexandria after the bombardment, the effect of their fire upon the wild mob of fanatic incendiaries and looters was quite extraordinary. These guns were not fired at the people, but a little over their heads, as a massacre would have been the result, had the guns been steadily trained at the mob. The rain of bullets, which they heard screaming over their heads,

produced a moral effect not easily described. I asked an Egyptian officer, some weeks afterwards, how on earth it was that Arabi and his 9,000 regular troops, who were within five miles, did not march down upon the town in the first four days after the bombardment, when Arabi knew that Captain Fisher's Naval Brigade, which held the lines, numbered less than 400 men. The Egyptian officer replied 'that he knew of no army which could face machines which "pumped lead", and that all the gates were defended by such machines' ... (Quoted in Wahl & Toppel 1966: 103)

From Alexandria, the British moved on to seize the Suez Canal, where another engagement featured Gatlings in the foretops of ships, as reported in the *London News* of 22 August 1882:

I have returned from Chalouf, fourteen miles up the Canal, where I witnessed the conclusion of a fight in which 250 men, including the 72nd. Highlanders, with the blue jackets and marines from the gunboats *Seagull* and *Mosquito*, brilliantly defeated a force twice their number. The fighting lasted from eleven until nearly five. The Gatling guns, in the tops of the gunboats, worked with admirable precision, doing much execution among the enemy, who had advanced to within 100 yards of the Canal bank.

On 2 September 1882 the *Broad Arrow*, a newspaper specially produced for the armed services, reported:

On all sides it is acknowledged that the Gatling has proved itself an effective arm of service to the present campaign. At Chalouf, and at

While at Alexandria, the commander of the Naval Brigade, Captain Fisher of HMS *Inflexible*, devised and supervised the construction of an armoured train, consisting of six wagons with the locomotive in the middle. The men and equipment in each truck were protected by iron plates and sandbags; at the front was a Nordenfelt gun and in the rear truck, three Gatlings. Other trucks held artillery along with Royal Marines. The train also carried equipment for laying and destroying rails. Here, we see the rear truck of the armoured train with its Gatling in readiness. This is one of the few contemporary views of a Naval Brigade Gatling which clearly shows the central dip in the axle and the absence of a seat on the trail of the carriage. *Illustrated London News*, 12 August 1882, p. 157. (Private collection)

Mahuta, the naval Gatling was admirably served by our blue jackets, and afforded 'invaluable assistance'. Indeed, it may be broadly affirmed that, in the encounter with the enemy at the former place, the results attained were chiefly ascribable to the action of the Gatlings from the tops of the gunboats *Seagull* and *Mosquito*. One hundred and sixty-eight Egyptian soldiers, out of 600, which composed the outpost, were placed 'hors-de-combat'. Under these circumstances, it is not unlikely that Sir Garnet Wolseley will employ Gatling batteries extensively in future operations.

A decisive battle commenced on 12 September 1882, when the British forces, numbering around 15,000 after the arrival of reinforcements, were able to attack the Egyptian stronghold at Tel-el-Kebir, manned by an estimated 38,000 troops and 60 pieces of artillery. It was a night attack, beginning at 11pm, and by 6am, Egyptian resistance had ended. British losses were 58 killed and 399 wounded or missing. The Egyptian losses, even inside a fortified position, were far greater, at nearly 2,000 killed and 500 wounded. One jubilant report, in the *Army and Navy Gazette* of 14 October 1882, states:

> the Naval machine gun battery, consisting of six Gatlings, manned by thirty seamen, reached the position assigned to it in the English lines on September 10th, and on Tuesday, September 12th, received orders to advance. They came within easy range of the Tel-el-Kebir earthworks, and observed guns in front, guns to the right, guns to the left, and a living line of fire above them. Nothing daunted, the order 'action front' was given, and was taken up joyously by every gun's crew. Round whisked the Gatlings, r-r-r-r-r-rum! r-r-r-r-r-rum! r-r-r-r-r-rum! that hellish noise the soldier so much detests in action, not for what it has done, so much as what it could do, rattled out. The report of the machine guns, as they rattle away, rings out clearly on the morning air. The

Port Said, founded at the mouth of the Suez Canal at the commencement of the excavation work on 25 April 1859, grew into one of Egypt's major cities and it was here that reinforcements from England were landed. Needless to say the city was fortified, although there was nothing like the same disturbances as in Alexandria, and again Gatlings were part of that defensive system. Here, men of the Naval Brigade and Marines defend the entrance to Port Said against incursion by the rebels. The reputation developed by the Gatling among the Egyptians in Alexandria no doubt also meant its very presence in the street was a sufficient deterrent against any show of unrest. *Illustrated London News*, 16 September 1882, p. 300. (Private collection)

parapets are swept. The embrasures are literally plugged with bullets. The flashes cease to come from them. With a cheer the blue jackets double over the dam, and dash over the parapet, only just in time to find their enemy in full retreat. That machine gun was too much for them.

Even before the problems in Egypt had erupted, there were rumblings of unrest in the Sudan. The self-proclaimed Mahdi, the 'divine guide', of Islam, Mohammed Ahmed, led his followers in a revolt. They were victorious over the British and Egyptians at El Obeid in 1883 but at the battle of El Teb on 29 February 1884, British forces overcame them. Examination of the rebel positions showed Krupp field guns and Gatlings captured in previous engagements. Almost a year later, part of a British force of approximately 1,400 men en route to relieve Major-General Charles G. Gordon who was besieged in Khartoum were engaged by around 5,000 Mahdists near Abu Klea. The battle which followed inspired Sir Henry Newbolt's famous poem 'Vitaï Lampada'. While a moving and inspired poem, it is factually incorrect; there were no Gatlings – the Naval Brigade was equipped with a Gardner gun which did jam, possibly due to sand getting into the mechanism, and the square, although shaken, did not break. The Mahdists were driven off after losing almost 1,000 dead. But after failing to save Gordon or Khartoum, Britain left the Sudan in the hands of the Mahdists.

There were other occasions in which the Gatling was used by British and colonial forces but they were largely small rebellions, such as the North West Rebellion by Louis Riel in Canada in 1885 (see Carol 1999). They also appeared again on the North West Frontier of India in the Black Mountain Expedition of 1888. A body of Ghazis, who had been concealed, made a desperate attempt to break through the line and were shot down by the infantry and Gatlings. This probably represents the last occasion on which a Gatling was used by British forces.

As the caption to this sketch reads: 'The Naval Brigade with Gatling and Gardner Guns hard at it at the Battle of Teb'. Following the victory at Tel-el-Kebir, the British rapidly moved 65 miles to assault Cairo and on 14 September, the Egyptian forces surrendered. Shortly after that, all renegade forces in Egypt gave up their struggle and Britain was in full control of the country and Arabi and the other nationalist leaders were sent to exile in Ceylon (modern Sri Lanka). *Illustrated London News*, 22 March 1884, p. 272. (Private collection)

IMPACT
'A terrible gun which shoots all day'

BATTLEFIELD IMPACT

The widespread use of the Gatling across the globe shows that it had a profound impact on military thinking at the time by simply introducing a new type of weapon. Even so, it also created confusion in the military mind. An inordinate amount of time seems to have been spent, probably because it was on a wheeled carriage, on trying to work out whether it should be considered as 'artillery' and where it might fall within that category of

Here, a US police patrol is equipped with a 'bulldog' Gatling, possibly advance publicity for the Model 1893 gun proposed as the 'Police Gatling'. According to *Scientific American* of 19 March 1892, it was named from 'its admirable adaptation for police or mounted service, for guarding railway trains, banks, or safe deposit institutions, or for use on vessels, yachts and boats'. It had 12in barrels, had the crank handle fitted at the rear and in .45-70 calibre fed from a scaled-down Accles drum capable of 800 rounds per minute. It seems an extreme measure for use in a civilian environment and only a few were sold, but it perhaps foreshadowed the problems that were to arise in the 'Roaring Twenties' when police and federal authorities had to combat machine-gun-wielding criminals. *Scientific American*, 19 March 1892. (Private collection)

weapon and how it should be deployed. Such an outlook wasted the gun's real potential and that was the real problem – there was no textbook guide or established practice which determined how such guns were to be used. It required imagination at a time when imagination was not something encouraged in military actions. It is interesting to note that, in Britain, while the Army was trying to decide who should control the Gatlings, the Royal Navy was the first service actually to use them in earnest!

The attitude of suppressing creative military thinking, or perhaps the confusion caused by a new weapon system, is possibly best exemplified by the failure of the French *mitrailleur* to meet the vaunted expectations of it. This was not because of mechanical or ballistic failings but because, as a new development in France's arsenal, it was kept so secret that the French high command seem to have forgotten to train anyone in its mechanical and tactical handling for its use on the field of battle. But although the *mitrailleur* of the French was not a rapid-firing gun in the sense of the Gatling, it was a multifiring rifle-calibre gun on a wheeled carriage and therefore had the same potential for deployment. Even disregarding that element of comparison, they did have Gatlings as well but for whatever reason they seem less worthy of mention so accounts of their use are virtually non-existent, or at least made difficult to find because of that all-embracing and confusing term, *mitrailleur*, which clouds most attempts at pinpointing which gun was being used. But, whether they were using *mitrailleurs* of the French type or the Gatling, they both presented the same questions of tactical employment, and the opportunity to rewrite, or at least add new chapters to the textbooks, was missed.

Gatling's concept of his new weapon perhaps being a deterrent to warfare was to some extent achieved in the Third Anglo-Ashanti War. Although the Gatling was never fired in anger, a demonstration of its capabilities, the like of which had never been seen before, acted as so much of a deterrent that it drove one Ashanti dignitary to commit suicide. However, it failed as a deterrent in the 'Battle of Liberty Place' in New Orleans the following year; the crowd still charged but there is no record that the Gatlings had fired. Had they done so, instead of 38 killed and 79 wounded, the outcome might have been far, far worse. In the Indian Wars, the Anglo-Zulu War and the Second Anglo-Afghan War, in the hands of Western armies the Gatlings were pitted against a foe no less brave but far less well equipped. Under such circumstances the Gatlings could hardly fail, but assessment of their effectiveness has to be balanced against the nature of the foe – in the Anglo-Zulu War, for instance, the Zulus did charge the Gatlings and got to within yards of them, but were also aware of their power and so attacked less well-defended quarters. That in itself speaks of the Gatling's effectiveness, but while the guns for the most part performed well and did what was expected of them, it would be difficult to form a balanced judgement of their effectiveness simply on these instances. However, in the Russo-Turkish War, where both sides were comparably equipped as regards firearms, and probably artillery also, the Gatlings showed their worth. Likewise in the Egyptian and Sudanese campaigns, the European armaments were closely matched by those of the opponents, but by this time the Gatling had been joined by other weapons

such as Gardners and Nordenfelts; these have to share any accolades, apart from known instances where Gatlings alone were employed. And once again, in a civil situation, the Gatling showed its value as an effective deterrent and means of crowd dispersal on the streets of Alexandria.

Yes, the British Gatlings did occasionally jam, but this was usually due to faulty ammunition feed from the Broadwell drum, or later from the Accles drum, especially if they had become damaged in some way. It has been noted that cartridges in the Broadwell drum could be tilted almost vertically if the drum was severely jolted in transit, a happening difficult to avoid on many of the roads in the regions where the British used them. It may be noteworthy that most Gatlings used in American actions favoured the simple hopper or 'feed box' arrangement, or the alternative Bruce feed system which seemed to suffer little jamming or derangement.

A US Gatling gun of the 6th Artillery is pictured in early August 1898 driving insurgents out of the brush at Pasay in the Philippine Islands, in an engagement during the Spanish–American War. Note the Bruce feed system in use, and the soldier on the left inserting new cartridges from their packing box. One half of a stereo photograph published in 1899 by Underwood & Underwood, New York, London, Toronto & Kansas. (Private collection)

It is perhaps during the Spanish–American War, in which both sides were armed with modern weapons, that the effectiveness of the Gatling can really be judged. Here the weapon was used with imagination and, functioning as mobile infantry support during the attack rather than being retired to a purely defensive role, helped to establish the future role of machine guns in warfare. As 1st Lieutenant John Parker, commander of one of the Gatling batteries, noted, 'To gain a flank and pour a sharp and unexpected fire upon the enemy is usually a decisive maneuver, and one particularly adapted to these guns' (quoted in Wahl & Toppel 1966: 82). In fairness, an element of this was seen in the Anglo-Zulu War when Midshipman Coker moved his guns the better to support the British infantry in their repulsion and pursuit of the attackers at Nyezane.

Of course, there are two famous instances of the non-use of Gatlings, thousands of miles apart but close in time and identical in outcome, where one cannot but wonder what their impact might have been. What if Custer had taken his Gatling with him on that fateful day in 1876 when the US Army's 7th Cavalry met the Sioux and Cheyenne at the Little Bighorn in one of the Native Americans' last armed efforts to preserve their way of life? What if Lord Chelmsford had taken his Gatlings on that momentous occasion in 1879 at Isandlwana when the British Army met the Zulu in battle? In both instances, the result of not wishing to be impeded by having Gatlings in tow was that a military force, heavily outnumbered by a poorly armed but brave and well-trained foe, was annihilated.

TECHNICAL INFLUENCE

Rivals and successors

The mechanical and military success of the Gatling gun served to inspire many other inventors to create different ways of achieving mechanized gunfire, but the only ones that achieved any degree of success were the Hotchkiss revolving cannon and the Nordenfelt and Gardner multifiring guns, all of which appeared around the same time.

The first was the Nordenfelt, which received UK patent no. 1,739 in 1873. In reality, though the weapon was named after him, Thorsten Nordenfelt was simply the man with the money; the gun was the brainchild of three Swedish engineers, Helge Palmcrantz, Johan Théodor Winborg and Eric Unge. The weapon was available in rifle calibre or a 1in-calibre version firing brass-cased steel bullets; mounted on a pedestal secured to the deck and firing steel projectiles, the latter was favoured for naval use as an anti-torpedo-boat weapon.

In 1874, William Gardner of Toledo, Ohio invented a rifle-calibre multifiring gun, again operated by a crank handle on the side. It came in various configurations with mountings for naval and land service. Mechanically, its 'bolts' were operated by revolving cams inside the casing and fitted on the crank-handle shaft and with one cam per bolt. With each revolution of the cam, a bolt fed a cartridge, delivered from an overhead-feed system, into the chamber of the barrel, fired it, and then extracted the empty case.

The Hotchkiss Revolving Cannon also first appeared around 1874 and although it looked like a Gatling, its mechanical functioning was completely different. It is curious that although it was built and sold under the Hotchkiss name, its basic mechanism would seem to have been invented and patented by Lewis Broadwell, Gatling's European agent (UK patent no. 250 of 1871). The Hotchkiss was designed expressly to be capable of firing explosive ammunition, with calibres ranging from 37mm to 57mm. Even the smallest was a heavy gun but, in addition to field carriage, it was offered with a pintle mounting to fit on the gunwale of a ship.

A single-barrelled Nordenfelt – perhaps a portent of the future with soldiers individually equipped with a machine gun instead of a rifle. Unlike many other rapid-fire guns at this time, the drive was not by means of a rotating crank but by a hand lever moved backwards and forwards. From Nordenfelt 1884, plate XLVIII, facing p. 161. (Private collection)

71

As far as Britain was concerned, the Gardner and Nordenfelt guns gradually found more favour. Both guns in .45in calibre, available with various numbers of barrels up to ten, were lighter in weight than the Gatling and therefore easier to manipulate in the field. Other countries adopted the Hotchkiss revolving cannon for field and naval use. Unlike the Gatling or the Hotchkiss, the Gardner and Nordenfelt guns came in various barrel configurations, from one to ten arranged in a flat row similar to an 'organ gun' and while the multibarrelled versions were quite heavy, the single-barrel version was light enough to be carried by one man. Various mountings were available including field carriage, tripod and pedestal for ships' decks, and the ammunition feed was by means of a vertical hopper. In many countries, these guns were destined to eclipse the Gatling by the end of the 19th century since, on the one hand they offered greater firepower, and on the other, a degree of versatility not possible with the Gatling.

A two-barrelled Gardner gun on a tripod. With an all-bronze casing for the mechanism and – in some cases like this – with the barrels encased in a bronze jacket with vents for air cooling, they were visually very striking. *Century Magazine*, Vol. XXXVI, May–October 1888, p. 887. (Private collection)

By this time, of course, with Hiram Maxim's first application of the power of recoil to drive the cycling of a gun, all hand-powered rapid-fire guns were effectively rendered obsolete. Maxim's 1883 patent of the true 'machine gun', in which the cyclic process of loading and firing was carried out automatically using a mechanism powered by recoil, meant the only physical exertion required of a gunner was to aim and actuate a

A Hotchkiss Revolving Cannon on field carriage from a Hotchkiss Company advertising handbook printed in Paris in 1879. (Private collection)

trigger. Even so, it should also be remembered that during the Spanish–American War, Gatlings were being used alongside the Browning-designed Colt Model 1895 fully automatic machine guns, a true test of the Gatling's perceived value and effectiveness.

Developing the Gatling concept

Throughout the weapon's period of use, Gatling – and others – were keen to correct any faults that arose and generally refine and improve the guns. We see the development of different systems for feeding ammunition into the gun which aided their performance and efficiency, in other words reduced any tendency to jam while increasing the rate of fire. We see the development of automatic traversing systems to give a spread of fire; we have the development of different mounting systems to suit different contexts of the gun's employment, from field carriages to tripods, all of which have become accepted standard features of many guns of today.

Faced with Maxim's patent, some attempts were made to devise means of converting the Gatling to automatic operation. Two in particular involved means of bleeding off the explosion gases and using their pressure to drive the mechanism. In one – patented by Carl J. Ehbets as US patent no. 550,262 of 1895 – small holes at the muzzles, as the barrel cluster revolved, were brought into alignment with a pad, which fitted over them in the same manner as the pads operated by remote keys on an instrument like a flute, attached to a lever forming part of a ratchet system. As the gases vented through the hole against the pad, the lever was pushed away and activated a ratchet system which rotated the gun and fired the next barrel which was now adjacent to the actuating pad. Another – patented by W.E. Simpson as UK patent no. 3,887 of 1896 – had the gases being vented from the barrel inside the casing and impinging on a series of pockets so that the barrel cluster rotated like the rotor of a turbine. If any of these guns were built, they never advanced beyond the experimental stage. But then, who needed such an ingenious way for the wholesale consumption of ammunition?

The only really successful experiment for alternative operation was recorded in *Scientific American* on 15 November 1890 when, at the invitation of the US Navy, the Crocker-Wheeler Electric Motor Company of New York fitted an electric motor to a Gatling fitted with an Accles feed and a clutch that allowed the gun to be electrically or manually operated. Even geared down, a rate of fire of 1,500 rounds per minute was achieved. In 1893 Gatling himself designed and patented a gun with an electric motor fitted inside an extended breech casing and whose spindle connected directly with the main shaft and was capable of firing 3,000 rounds per minute (US patent no. 502,185 of 1893 and UK patent no. 14,749 of 1893). Here, we see a detail from Gatling's UK patent no. 14,749 of 1893, showing the extended lock casing to the left, housing an electric motor with direct drive to the main shaft of the gun. These very high rates of fire reflect the degree of refinement which had been brought to the mechanism and which allowed them to function at such high speed. (Private collection)

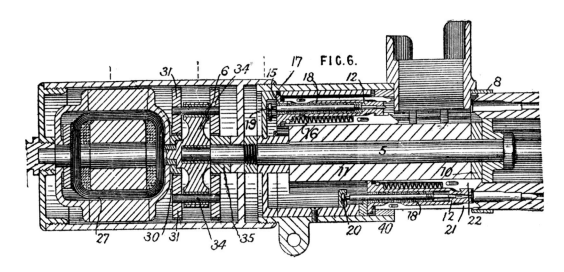

73

That need for a very high rate of fire did arise in the aftermath of World War II with, initially, the advent of jet fighters. Their speed meant a target only appeared in their sights for seconds and the highest rate of fire obtainable with a conventional machine gun was too low to give the volume of fire necessary to give any chance of hitting it. To achieve the rate of fire needed, the electrically driven Gatling was resurrected as the basis for Project Vulcan. The success has led to the creation of a variety of weapons, ranging in calibre from 7.62mm 'minigun' to 30mm 'vulcans' for land, sea and air use and capable of cyclic rates of 6,000 and higher. Their effect is devastating, whatever the target. The volume of fire – the number of projectiles in the air in almost any instant – is sufficiently dense that they can be used effectively against missiles. World War II showed how difficult it was to hit even a relatively slow-moving missile such as the V 1 with fully automatic artillery firing explosive shells fitted with proximity fuses, but, with modern fire-control and aiming systems, it is a task the electric descendants of the Gatling with their focussed and concentrated firepower can do with ease.

Aviation Ordnanceman Airman Eric Young inspects a 20mm Vulcan gun removed from an F/A-18F Super Hornet, assigned to the Diamondbacks of Strike Fighter Squadron One Zero Two (VFA-102). The Vulcan gun, the modern large-calibre equivalent of the Gatling, is capable of firing 6,000 rounds per minute or higher. Because of the restricted weight of ammunition that can be carried in an aircraft – often insufficient for 1 minute of firing – they are restricted to short bursts. Even so, when equipped with laser and GPS targeting technology and firing armour-piercing and explosive incendiary rounds, they are truly formidable weapons. (US Navy)

CONCLUSION

The widespread use of the Gatling shows that there were those who recognized that it brought to the battlefield a new type of weapon capable of devastating performance if used appropriately and correctly. Gatling's own reasons for creating it in the first place, as a means of saving human life and suffering on the battlefield, are perhaps somewhat fatuous; it did not save the lives of the army which faced it, only of that which wielded it! The Gatling gun also had a deterrent value to some extent. Its effect on the minds of the Ashanti warlords was dramatic to say the least! However, it may have failed as a deterrent halfway across the globe on the streets of New Orleans a year or so later but that may be the result of knowing it would not actually be used against fellow citizens – so the crowds still charged. Swinging back to North Africa a decade after that, its 'crowd control' abilities were demonstrated again in suppressing or preventing riots in Alexandria and Port Said. Its crowd-control potential even led to its suggested use by American police in certain quarters.

It also caused confusion in the military mind which, like any bureaucratic government department, has an enormous momentum of tradition to overcome before direction can be changed. Gradually, that thinking was changed and, in becoming seen as an infantry-support weapon instead of a branch of artillery, the Gatling and its later sisters paved the way for the lighter and more mobile fully automatic weapons introduced by Maxim and others.

Even in the era of the fully automatic guns, the Gatling still found its place. It was used alongside the Colt-Browning machine gun in the Spanish–American War. But soon it became redundant, old technology cast aside in the face of new. But its story was not over. Newer technology in aircraft – the rise of the jet – at the end of World War II demanded something better than the best of what by then had become 'traditional' machine guns, something capable of much higher rates of fire to keep pace with speeding jets or to provide a barrage capable of shattering missiles or other targets. The Gatling was resurrected, driven by electric motors and capable of phenomenal rates of fire, to become the Vulcan Gun, the Minigun, the 'Magic Dragon' in the film *The Green Berets*, and others. That it could be resurrected to become a powerful weapon in the modern arsenal speaks volumes for the genius embodied in its basic principles. But in extolling the mechanical virtues, we should not lose sight of the fact that it was one of the earliest forerunners of automated killing.

But perhaps the greatest compliment paid to any invention in acknowledging its status is its appearance in fiction and as far as rapid-fire guns of any description are concerned, the Gatling is probably the first: '"Oh, for a gatling!" groaned Good as he contemplated the serried phalanx beneath us. "I would clear that plain in twenty minutes"' (Rider Haggard 1907: 101) and that is what the Gatling was all about.

A British Army sentinel beside one of the Gatlings at Ginginlovu. *Illustrated London News*, 7 June 1879, p. 525. (Private collection)

GLOSSARY

CAM: The spiral groove on the inside of the lock casing into which fits a nib or lug on the lock so that, as the main shaft, on which is fixed the barrel and lock assembly, rotates, the lock is forced to reciprocate in the lock carrier.

CARTRIDGE CARRIER: A cylindrical block fixed on the main shaft forward of the lock carrier with suitably shaped troughs on the outer periphery which are aligned with the centre lines of the locks in the lock carrier, and of the barrels, and into which the cartridges fall from the feed system and in which the locks reciprocate during the operation of the gun.

CASCABLE: Originally referred to the large knob or button at the breech end of a cannon and later the whole portion of which the button forms part; in the case of the Gatling, the cascable plate is the part of the breech casing which carries the cascable.

COCKING CAM: A smaller cam which engages a projection on the hammer or striker when the breech is closed, withdrawing and then releasing it to fire the cartridge. While each lock is in continuous engagement with the main cam, its striker is only intermittently engaged with the cocking cam.

CRADLE or YOKE: An approximately 'Y'-shaped component with sockets at the top of the two arms into which the trunnions of the gun frame can fit.

DIAPHRAGM: A circular plate inside the lock casing which separates the lock mechanism from the driving mechanism and provides the rear bearing for the mainshaft.

ELEVATING GEAR: Gear used to tilt the axis of the gun in the vertical plane.

GUN FRAME: A pair of suitably machined wrought iron bars fitted to each side of the lock casing and connected at the front by the double-humped bridge-piece.

HAMMER: The original term for the spring-loaded component which struck the percussion cap in the first guns. In later guns which were built to use metallic cartridges, the 'hammer' was fitted with a firing pin and its more modern term would be 'striker'.

LoC: List of Changes in War Matériel and Patterns of Military Stores, often just abbreviated to 'List of Changes'. These give a fascinating insight into the variety of military equipment used by the British armed services.

LOCK: In the Gatling gun the reciprocating part which contains the striker and mainspring and which is used to feed and withdraw cartridges from the chamber and act as a breech-block. The more modern term would probably be 'bolt', in comparison with a bolt-action rifle.

LOCK CARRIER: A cylindrical block fixed on the main shaft with suitable apertures to carry the locks/bolts and allow them to reciprocate freely as they interact with the various cams.

LOCK CASING: The cylindrical hollow cast iron or bronze case surrounding and protecting the lock mechanism, housing the gears which allow the gun to be operated with the crank handle, providing support for the rear end of the mainshaft. It is closed at the rear end by the **cascable** (qv) plate. Two ribs on the side of the lock casing are used to securely bolt the casing to the **gun frame** (qv).

MAINSHAFT: The central shaft to which are fixed in correct alignment relative to each other the driving gear, lock carrier, cartridge carrier, and cluster of barrels.

MOUNTING: Various forms of mounting were used; the typical wheeled carriage similar to an artillery carriage; a heavy conical metal mounting fixed to a ship's deck; a tripod; a cradle fitted with a pintle, or cylindrical spigot, which could be fitted into a socket on the gunwale or other part of a ship.

RSAF: Royal Small Arms Factory at Enfield, just outside London.

TRAVERSING GEAR: The equipment or mechanism used to swing the axis of the gun from side to side, either manually or automatically.

TRUNNIONS: Two short cylindrical projections from the gun frame or other integral component used to set the gun in a mounting and allow it to pivot in a vertical plane.

BIBLIOGRAPHY

There are few books devoted to the Gatling gun – probably only five in the last 50 years. Why that should be is a mystery considering the status it has achieved. Its appearance in print before the 1960s was largely confined to the last quarter of the 19th century in official documents, reports of various committees in the United States and Britain, and possibly in other countries also, but they have not been located. These reports, both governmental and the various journals of military related societies with both technical commentary and accounts of the use in battle, plus various newspapers of the period are documents not readily come by outside specialist and national libraries.

Admiralty (1877). *Handbook for the 0.45-Inch Gatling Gun for Naval Service*. London: HMSO.

Adye, Major-General Sir John, KCMG, CB (1925). *Soldiers and Others I have Known*. London: Herbert Jenkins.

Armstrong, David A. (1982). *Bullets and Bureaucrats: The Machine Gun and the United States Army 1861–1916*. Westport, CT: Greenwood Publishing.

Baring, Captain E. (1874). 'The Bavarian "revolver cannon"'. In *Minutes of the Proceedings of the Royal Artillery Institution*, Vol. 8: 28–30.

Beresford, Captain the Rt Hon. Lord Charles W.D., RN (1884). 'Machine guns in the field'. In *Royal United Services Institution Journal*, Vol. 28, Issue 127: 941–63.

Brockett, L.P. (1871). *The Year of Battles*. New York, NY: J.W. Goodspeed & Co.

Brown, Lieutenant-Colonel J.T.B. (1881). 'An account of the march of Lord Chelmsford's column to Ulundi, in June and July, 1879'. In *Minutes of the Proceedings of the Royal Artillery Institution*, Vol. 11: 146–58.

Carol, Lindon (1999). *Gatling Guns at the North West Rebellion*. Edmonton: Shorthorn Press.

Carson, Kevin (2011). *The Long Journey of the Nez Perce: A Battle History from Cottonwood to the Bear Paw*. Yardley, PA: Westholme Publishing.

Chinn, Lieutenant Colonel G.M. (1951). *The Machine Gun: History, evolution, and development of manual, automatic, and airborne repeating weapons*. Washington, DC: Government Printing Office.

Committee on Machine Guns (1880). *Second Progress Report*. London: HMSO.

Cowan's Auctions, Inc. (2007). Auction catalogue, 7 November 2007, auction lot 279.

Cruse, J. Brett (2008). *Battles of the Red River War: Archeological perspectives on the Indian campaign of 1874*. College Station, TX: Texas A&M University Press.

Featherstone, Donald F. (1978). *Weapons and equipment of the Victorian soldier*. Poole: Blandford Press.

Fletcher, Lieutenant-Colonel H.C. (1872). 'The employment of mitrailleurs during the recent war and their use in future wars'. In *Royal United Services Institution Journal*, Vol. 16, Issue 66: 28–57.

Fosbery, Major G.V., VC (1869). 'On Mitrailleurs, and their place in the Wars of the Future'. In *Royal United Services Institution Journal*, Vol. 13, Issue 56: 539–63.

Fullam, William F. & Hart, Thomas C. (1903). *Text-book of Ordnance and Gunnery*. Annapolis, MD: United States Naval Institute.

Gatling, R.J. (1870). 'Machine guns; the "Gatling Battery" – the Agar and Claxton guns – the French and Montigny mitrailleurs'. In *Royal United Services Institution Journal*, Vol. 14, Issue 60: 504–28.

Hamilton, Alexander (1827). *Report on the Subject of Manufactures*. 6th Edition. Philadelphia, PA: William Brown.

Hamilton, Lieutenant William R. (1888). 'American Machine Cannon and Dynamite Guns'. In *The Century Magazine*, Vol. XXXVI, October 1888: 885–93.

Hotchkiss, B.B. (1880). 'On Hotchkiss' Revolving Guns'. In *Royal United Services Institution Journal*, Vol. 24, Issue 105: 279–97.

Hughes, James B. (2000). *The Gatling Gun Notebook: A Collection of Data and Illustrations.* Lincoln, RI: Mowbray, Inc.

Keller, Julia (2008). *Mr Gatling's Terrible Marvel.* London: Viking Penguin.

Landry, Stuart Omer (1955). *The Battle of Liberty Place: The overthrow of carpet-bag rule in New Orleans September 14, 1874.* New Orleans, LA: Pelican Publishing.

Lloyd, Lt W.N., RHA (1881). 'The defence of Ekowe'. In *Minutes of the Proceedings of the Royal Artillery Institution*, Vol. 11: 451–65.

Lock, R. & Quantrill, P. (2005). *Zulu Vanquished: The destruction of the Zulu Kingdom.* London: Greenhill Books.

Marvin, Commander J.D. (1875). *Instructions for the Use and Care of Naval Gatling Guns.* Washington, DC: Government Printing Office.

Minutes, Director of Artillery and Stores, London, 1870. Minute no. 2873.

Molyneux, Major-General W.C.F. (1896). *Campaigning in South Africa and Egypt.* London: Macmillan & Co.

Report from Captain Noble of Sir W.G. Armstrong & Co. to the Special Committee on Mitrailleurs, recorded in *Proceedings of the Department of the Director of Artillery*, 14 March 1871, Minute 29174, p. 163 *et seq.*

Nordenfelt, Thorsten (1884). *The Nordenfelt Machine Guns, Described in Detail and Compared with other Systems; also their Employment for Naval and Military Purposes.* Portsmouth: Griffin & Co.

Norton, Brevet Brigadier General Charles B. (1880). *American Inventions and Improvements in Breech-Loading Small Arms, Heavy Ordnance, Machine Guns, Magazine Arms, Fixed Ammunition, Pistols, Projectiles, Explosives, and Other Munitions of War, including a Chapter on Sporting Arms.* Springfield, MA: Chapin & Gould.

Ordnance Department (1874). Ordnance Memorandum No. 17. 'Report of a Board of Officers on Gatling Guns of Large Caliber for Flank Defense'. p. 18. Washington, DC: Government Printing Office.

Ordnance Department (1917). *Handbook, Gatling Gun, Caliber .30: Models of 1895, 1900, and 1903.* Washington, DC: Government Printing Office.

Parker, John H. (1898). *The Gatlings at Santiago.* Kansas City, Kansas: Hudson Kimberley Publishing Co.

Parker, 1st Lieutenant John H. (1899). *Tactical organization and uses of machine guns in the field.* Kansas City, Kansas: Hudson Kimberly Publishing Co.

Potomac Corral of the Westerners (1966). *Great Western Indian Fights.* Lincoln, NE: Bison Books.

Rider Haggard, Henry (1907). *King Solomon's Mines.* London, Paris, New York, Toronto & Melbourne: Cassell & Co., Ltd.

Rogers, Captain E., FRGS (1875). 'The Gatling Gun; its place in tactics'. In *Royal United Services Institution Journal*, Vol. 19, Issue 82: 419–45.

Ruble, Ron (2009). *Gatling Gun Patent Drawings.* Place of publication not known: Ron Ruble Enterprises.

Stephenson, E. Frank, Jr. (1993). *Gatling: A photographic remembrance.* Murfreesboro, NC: Meherrin River Press.

Wahl, Paul & Toppel, Donald R. (1966). *The Gatling Gun.* London: Herbert Jenkins.

War Office (1877). *Treatise on the Construction and Manufacture of Ordnance in the British Service.* London: HMSO.

War Office (1880). *Handbook for the 0.45 Inch Gatling Gun for Land Service.* 3rd edition. London: HMSO.

War Office (1887). *Treatise on Ammunition.* 4th edition. London: HMSO.

War Office (1893). *Treatise on Service Ordnance.* 4th edition. London: HMSO.

INDEX